God's Healing Power Through You

Copyright
Paul and Lynn Crawford

ISBN978-1-4276-3830-4

Published by
New Sound Media
PO Box 7300, Kingston, WA

godshealingpower@gmail.com

Acknowledgements and Thanks

God has used many wonderful people to pray for us and keep us along the Way. Space makes it impossible to list all of you, so please forgive us if you aren't mentioned here. We really appreciate all your love and prayers.

When we lived at Friday Harbor, WA Tookie Estrada had an Aglow prayer meeting at her home that forged our hearts and lives together forever. Rose, Linda, Patty, Joey and Mary and of course Took, I'm so grateful for you all. North Sound Women's Aglow, thank you for helping prepare me for ministry. Our Pastor, in Friday Harbor, Fr. Ted Leche and his wife Mary Jane. We love you and were blessed to have you officiate when we renewed our wedding vows on our twenty fifth anniversary. Bob and Barbara Bignold and the Seattle FGBMFI really launched us into the nations in the 1980's.

The Happy Hunter's are amazing. Their love for Jesus and each other changed us and our marriage forever. Mike Bickle and the KC IHOP for their encouragement, and teaching us about intersession in a way we could participate fully.

When we moved to Bellevue, WA, Joe and Linda Knight were our beloved pastors at Cornerstone. I met Marilyn Pearson there my forever friend and life saver prayer partner extraordinaire! Many times when I couldn't hear God for myself, she had His Word for me. Mary Burris, Thunder Mary, another trumpet for God, with His Word and Strategy for us at crucial moments. We thank God for each of you.

We appreciate the support we've received from our pastors Scott and Leilani Montagne, Brent Hershey and our entire Bayside

Community Church family, especially the prayer warriors of the Adult Sunday School class.

We have grown as writers and appreciate the fellowship and help we've received from the North Kitsap Christian Writer's Group. Special thanks to Dee Kamp for all her editing and writing help.

I'm really grateful for my special tea friends. And especially my awesome anointed neighbor and best friend forever Gayle Johnson who loves me enough to listen to my insecurities for the first mile of our daily walks, but then helps me start believing God for the second mile and praise Him all the way home.

Thanks to David McDermott who fixed our errors and made this book read easier.

And finally, we want to thank our children who gave up many days with their parents so we could minister overseas. We are blessed God chose us to be your parents.

We especially thank God who created us in Christ Jesus to do beautiful good works, which He prepared in advance for us to do.

The grace of our Lord Jesus be with you as you read this book.

Blessings, The Crawfords

Unless otherwise indicated, all Scripture quotations are from the New Living Translation Bible. Holy Bible, New Living Translation ®, copyright © 1996, 2004 by Tyndale Charitable Trust. Used by permission of Tyndale House Publishers. All rights reserved.

CHAPTERS

	Page
1. The Awakening	8
2. GHPTY Seminar Overview	12
3. My Call	18
4. Learning to walk by Faith	24
5. Power of Agreement	36
6. Franco Set Free	50
7. Forgiveness	58
8. Divine Pardon	68
9. Loving Yourself God's Way	74
10. Faith Stretchers	78
11. The Catholic Connection	84
12. China	88
13. Sister Rosie's Creative Miracle	94
14. FGBMFI Japan	98
15. Creating a Healing Atmosphere: Praise	102
16. Categories of Healing	108
17. Ten Actions Until Your Healing Manifests	128
18. Declaring: Praying the Word	134
19. Declaring: Personalizing Healing and Health Scriptures	140
20. GHPT Seminar/Study Outline	194
21. The Happy Hunters	232

The Awakening

Paul Crawford

During my 30's, I was at best a carnal Christian. I believed but Jesus was not Lord of my life. I served my needs, wants and desires. After moving to a remote island, part of the Pacific North West San Juan Islands, my life slowed down. I worked for a famous national women's sportswear brand. My job was to sell to their clients in Washington, Oregon, Idaho and Montana. The job consisted of five selling periods in a year; each one being about five weeks long. After each period, I would have a five week break which allowed me some time off.

This gave me a chance to view my life from a new and fresh perspective, which allowed me to see that my spirit was in need. My wife Lynn had started attending a very small church, ten on a good Sunday. After some time I went with her, and I also attended some of the Full Gospel Businessmen's Fellowship International meetings in Seattle. Through these Seattle meetings I heard about a FGBMFI Conference in British Columbia, Canada. The meeting place was the Empress Hotel Victoria which was twelve air miles from my home in Roche Harbor, WA. I made a reservation to attend. I bought myself a big Bible like most of the Full Gospel Businessmen had. To get there I took a ferryboat from Friday Harbor, WA to Sydney, British Columbia. On the way to the ferry I stopped and picked up my mail. My new Playboy magazine arrived and I put it into my suitcase right next to my new very big Bible. My Christian walk was weak and without destiny and I didn't even consider my actions. The first night of the conference I asked Jesus Christ to become Lord of my life again.

The next morning there was a general meeting and in the afternoon, workshops. I chose to attend one of the workshops where Don Northrop of Maranatha Ministries spoke on "The Prophetic." After about thirty minutes of teaching he started operating by the Holy Spirit, in the gift of the Word of Knowledge. I knew about this gift but had never seen it in action. Don would ask someone to stand and would then tell them something about their life, and what God had for them in the future. I could tell by their reactions that God was showing Don intimate details about each individual's life.

Then it hit me, God showed him about my Playboy back at the hotel room. I had become so carnal in my nature, that it never crossed my mind not to bring the magazine with me. I had not opened it, but realized God knew everything about me and he had probably told Don. I sat through the rest of the afternoon in fear that he would call me out and expose my sins and my Playboy. This would be so embarrassing in front of such men of God. But to my relief, Don never called me out. Immediately, I rushed back to my hotel and put the Playboy magazine in the trash. I have never opened a Playboy since.

Regarding the issue of pornography, some may be offended by my frankness. As you know it has taken many national leaders down. If you decide to move from a pew warmer to ministry, we promote in this book that you need to be vigilant against the enemy's attacks by facing and ending them early. One of the highlights in a man's life is to be sexually stimulated physically and/or emotionally. This is tied to a man's ego, and generally this desire is ever present. For most this does not go away until death.

Today, Playboy and like magazines, have been greatly replaced by stimulation from advertising, television, the Internet and movies. Every man needs to guard his psyche, as well as his family against this issue. Vain imaginations enter a man's mind through his ego or from the enemy. If not put to death, vain imaginations will likely lead to moral failure. It's a battle against the enemy that is often lost without being vigilant. God can and will heal these areas.

The same evening of the Prophetic service, I lead a man into salvation for the first time in my life. That's an experience I will never forget. I saw him across the room and felt impressed to challenge him. I had never done this as I feared a question would be asked of me that I could not answer. Be confident, don't let that stop you. The Holy Spirit will have the answers. After the service, I watched some of the leaders of the FGBMFI minister to many. The most visual was the "growing out of legs" as it was referred to. People who had back pain were put in a chair. They were told to sit up straight and extend their legs out. The person ministering would measure their legs at the heel and show everybody the difference in length. They would pray that the leg grow and the pain go. In most cases, the leg seemed to grow and their pain was gone. This all seemed kind of silly to me. Later I found this ministry form was straightening and healing the lower back which caused a pelvic position change and would result in the legs being evened. Don't knock the ministry style if God is healing through the believers' efforts. All the great ministers of healing in the 40's and 50's had some ministry styles that many questioned. Some were not healed because they had put God in a box.

Over the past forty years, I have known God to be One who does miracles continually, in all aspects of life. For me, the Word of God has gone from head knowledge to spirit faith. My wife

Lynn and I have seen almost all diseases and sickness healed. Often these healings were people ministered to by a "God's Healing Power Through You" seminar trainee.

God's Healing Power Through You

Seminar Overview

Paul Crawford

I was raised in a Pentecostal Church where my father was the pastor. We believed that healing was for today and we prayed for the sick. I received the gift of the Baptism in the Holy Spirit at age 12. This took place at a summer outdoor meeting. I spoke in tongues for hours that night. I felt like I could burst. The stars in the sky were the most brilliant I had ever seen. The whole world was beautiful. All the people were beautiful. I had an unlimited love for everyone that night.

At age 27, I saw my first visible healing at a Kathryn Kuhlman meeting. Kathryn was known around the world for a ministry in the 1970's with significant healings. She held regular meetings in the USA, and was interested in videoing her services and asked me to study the ways is could be done discreetly. She was sensitive to and honored the Holy Spirit. Miss Kuhlman gave me free access to any place in the meeting auditorium or onstage. I was standing in the center aisle of the Shrine Auditorium in Los Angeles, CA when it happened. A young woman started to scream. As I looked at her, she was gazing at her mother whose hands were gnarled with arthritis. Popping and crackling noises were coming from the mother's hands as they straightened and became whole. All the swelling was gone and she was flexing them in unbelief. I saw many healings that day and more than 100 testimonies of God's healing power at work. For two years, I was at each monthly Shrine meeting. God healed people across the auditorium without any hype, or laying on of hands. She would lay hands on them after they were healed. I attended many of her crusades in other cities and had numerous personal meetings with Miss Kuhlman. This woman preached the Word, entered into extended Praise and Worship and honored and welcomed the Holy Spirit.

In 1984, I met Charles and Frances Hunter at a Full Gospel Business Men's convention in Tacoma, Washington. This was the first time the Hunters spoke at a FGBMFI event. Frances had previously been injured by a person who fell on her while she was praying for them so she asked me to accompany her as she went down the ministry line. Inches away, I saw the Holy Spirit move upon many people that would be overcome, transformed by God's touch, and receive healing. The Hunters were conducting meetings across the United States which they called "Healing Explosions." The following month, they invited me to one which took place in Pittsburg, PA. The meeting consisted of two days of training, and a one day healing service. For the first time I saw people healed on whom I had laid hands on. Over the next few years, my wife Lynn and I served Charles and Frances at meetings and training sessions in more than 20 cities. I then set up and coordinated their overseas "Healing Explosions" for three years in Tokyo, Osaka,

Taipei, Hong Kong, Canton, Kiev, Manila, Cebu, Copenhagen and more.

One of Charles and Frances' themes was: "If Charles and Frances can do it, so can you." Lynn and I heard it enough times that we started to believe it. We began conducting our own "Healing Explosions" that we called *"God's Healing Power Through You,"* where we followed the Hunters' pattern. Most of the people who took the training with the Hunters were the "Chairs-Maniac types" and most were well-grounded in the Word of God. The Hunters' teaching and training were based on the trainees' expected understanding of the Word. With *"God's Healing Power Through You,"* we had in mind more traditional Christians that may not have had a broad knowledge of the Bible. Our focus is on scripture dealing with healing and our individual response to the Word in action; our training program is designed to saturate Christians in the Word of God. As with the Hunters, our theme is found in

> *Mark 16:15-18: And then he told them, "Go into all the world and preach the Good News to everyone, everywhere. Anyone who believes and is baptized will be saved. But anyone who refuses to believe will be condemned.* **These signs will accompany those who believe: They will cast out demons in my name, and they will speak new languages.** *They will be able to handle snakes with safety, and if they drink anything poisonous, it won't hurt them.* **They will be able to place their hands on the sick and heal them."** (NLT)

I have studied this verse in 38 translations. One version says: **"Believers who Believe"** will lay hands on the sick and they will be healed. This has been my experience all over the world. This has been my experience with brand new Christians, and with older Christians who have been "re-ignited." Believers who believe will lay hands on the sick and they will be healed. Praise God! I have seen people—individuals who had never ministered before—lay hands on someone blind from birth and instantly their sight was restored 100%.

Our typical *"God's Healing Power Through You"* seminar is a three-day event held in conjunction with a group of churches. Our model has been developed from our personal experiences with individuals gifted in healing like Kathryn Kuhlman, Charles & Frances Hunter, John Wimber. Watching Benny Hinn, Kenneth Hagen and Oral Roberts minister as well as our study and research of John G. Lake, Smith Wigglesworth, William Branham and more; has impacted the assembling of our seminars. We usually do the teaching, training and demonstration Friday evening and all day Saturday, and then conduct a healing service on Sunday afternoon. After 12 hours of teaching and training focused on Faith, Healing, Jesus Christ's works, and His Commandments to all believers; trainees become **"Believers who BELIEVE."** A seminar contains six sessions that average two hours each and are a combination of teaching and demonstration. Many people have been dramatically healed during the demonstrations. After 12 hours in the Word and a unity of purpose, a corporate anointing comes upon the group that overcomes sickness, disease, oppression and all the works of the devil. Because our teaching is not limited to hearing, but also contains the doing of what God's Word tells us in Mark 16:17-18, we see God healing through ordinary Christians.

Ordinary Christians doing Extraordinary Works.

Bio

Paul and Lynn Crawford have been in fulltime lay ministry for 28 years and minister and teach as a team. Their ministry has extended throughout the world with more than 100 overseas trips, hundreds of conferences and the production of more than 9,000 videos. Their video ministry, International Television & Evangelism Center/www.OneInTheSpirit.tv is based in the Seattle area of Washington State.

Paul and Lynn's training and healing ministry experience was most impacted by a six-year association with Charles and Frances Hunter and a two-year relationship with Kathryn Kuhlman at the Los Angeles Shrine meetings.

They have witnessed thousands receiving healing through the people they trained around the world—healings from sicknesses that include Cancer, Blindness from Birth, MS, and the Crippled made whole. In the process, cities and churches have been impacted and its people energized.

Paul and Lynn live in Kingston, Washington on the Kitsap Peninsula; a ferry ride West of Seattle. Their home Church is Bayside Community Church located in Kingston. They have 6 children and many grandchildren.

My Call

Paul Crawford

I left a retail sales career in 1979 with a call from God on my life. Following a sales meeting in the Chicago Merchandise Mart, I took an elevator to the lobby. As I looked around, I noticed there was an exhibition hall having a video equipment show. I made up a name and registered as *PMC Video* (Paul M. Crawford) and entered the show. About 15 years prior to this time, while in college, I had previous television training with Settle Public Television. I was amazed at the great leaps of television technology.

While viewing the equipment God spoke into my spirit *"I Want You To Use Video to Spread the Gospel."* I have never questioned this was God's will for my life, even up to this day. The call was clear though the steps were not a defined path. At times, we have strayed from "His Perfect Will" while trying to find it, however I have never thought of giving up, nor did I falter. Every challenge has been a tool in our growth and an understanding of who our God is.

My primary calling is to use the medium of video in order to spread the Gospel, Teach, Train, and to bring Healing and Forgiveness.

Fulfilling this calling started with me applying for a television broadcast license with channel 24 in order to serve Seattle and Vancouver with Christian Television. The process took 6 years before being granted, and would have to be approved through the FCC. During this time, we kept busy with other ministry opportunities. Lynn and I had started a Youth Ministry in which we conducted events on the weekends. We also established an Israel Touring business in which we worked predominantly with Roman Catholics and brought many to a personal relationship with Christ. We brought fifteen different groups to the Holy Land in a period of 4 years. After our work with the Roman Catholics we assisted Charles and Francis with their "Healing Explosions," and I also became a FGBMFI field representative and was asked to search out and help establish chapters in Asia. At the same time, Charles & Francis Hunter asked me to help set up Healing Explosions in Asia. I was the forerunner for FGBMFI chapters in Japan, Taiwan and Shanghai. Healing Explosions were held in three Japanese cities; Taipei, Canton and Manila.

Also in the early years, I produced over 250 programs on the Seattle cable television system which had over 300,000 subscribers. One program was "Papa Chuck's Place." Fr. Chuck was a Spirit-filled Catholic priest. The set was in pizza pallor with tables that had red and white table cloths. As they ate their pizza, Fr. Chuck would ask each guest what God had done in their life.

In 1988, we were asked to substitute for the Hunters and speak at a Eurovision Conference in Karlsruhe Germany. Eurovision Conferences were established for Eastern Europeans-in the Cold War Days-to come to Germany and hear the Gospel as well as return home with resources and videos that were produced. We taught two afternoons training the attendees to minister healing as Christ had. This led us to teach a three day seminar in many of

Germany's largest churches. International Television & Evangelism Center (ITEC) was birthed at the Eurovision Conference. The sponsor of the video production from England was producing video tapes of each speaker and duplicating them immediately with his equipment-thirty-six VCRs. Eurovision attracted many Eastern Europe attendees, as the Conference Coordinator had a gift for acquiring visas. The Russian block countries, such as Romania, Bulgaria, Poland, would not allow Christian publications to be sent into their countries, but conference attendees were often allowed to bring them back on their return. The sponsor of the video production would get over a thousand videos per conference back to these countries however there was one big problem; the sponsor was going broke. I hired him and his English crew, and with his equipment, I did conferences in Germany, England, Switzerland, Denmark and Sweden. These included John Wimbers' Guttenberg, Sweden and Docklands London conferences.

In 1988, I also started my first of thirty-three trips to China. Being in Europe and China allowed Lynn and me to see history first hand. We were at the Berlin Wall when it came down and I was in Tiananmen Square the day before the tanks rolled in.

To date, I have produced media at over 700 conferences with 10,000 original video cassettes, audio cassettes, DVDs and CDs. Millions of copies have been distributed.

We have operated independently but not by choice. We could not find any ministry that would oversee our own. They didn't want to take a chance on our big dreams and likely failure. Throughout the nearly thirty years, God has supplied all our needs for family and ministry. Some of the ministries we have assisted have paid many of our travel costs. No church or ministry paid us or sponsored our personal needs. Some have provided some specific support, for instance, $700 for Bibles to China. Many individuals have provided substantial funds for our work and calling. The fact that we have operated independently has allowed us to quickly respond to missions we believe God assigned to us.

We are very excited about our ministry in the future years. I believe we will remain strong and productive for another 20 years. Our goal for 2008 was to finish writing *"God's Healing Power Through You"*. We have restarted our three-day seminar *"God's Healing Power Through You,"* and plan to conduct about 15-20 per year. We will continue our own video production and distribution and assist other ministries within our calling.

In 1995, just after the public birth of the Internet I wrote the vision statement:

To have a website webcasting conferences live from all over the world, high video quality, full screen, using software that would translate into eight languages representing 85% of the worlds understanding.

As the software develops, this vision will come alive. Currently I have a website, *www.OneInTheSpirit.tv* where I produce video and broadcast conferences live and on demand.

When we give up "our rights" and become His bond slave, God has the responsibility to take care of us. We have been bond slaves of our Master for a long time. We have a big GOD; our Healer, our Provider, our Lord, our Protector, our Joy and One who has shown us forgiveness, grace, mercy and love.

Today we hear God saying: **"Now Is The Time For The USA"**

Romans 13 : 11   "Besides this you know what [a critical] hour this is, how it is <u>high time</u> now for you to wake up out of your sleep (rouse to reality). For salvation (final deliverance) is nearer to us now than when we first believed (adhered to, trusted in, and relied on Christ, the Messiah)."

2 Cor. 6:2   For God says, "At just the right time, I heard you. On the day of salvation, I helped you." Indeed, the "right time" is now. Today is the day of salvation.

Heb. 1:1-3   Long ago God spoke many times and in many ways to our ancestors through the prophets. 2. And now in these final days, he has spoken to us through his Son. God promised everything to the Son as an inheritance, and through the Son he created the universe. 3. The Son radiates God's own glory and expresses the very character of God, and he sustains everything by the mighty power of his command. When he had cleansed us from our sins, he sat down in the place of honor at the right hand of the majestic God in heaven.

We are getting back to teaching our seminar. We expect to do fifteen in the USA and a few overseas in the next year. We will expand our ministries' outreach through the Internet and will continue media production.

Please pray for us.

Learning To

Walk By Faith

Lynn Crawford

     Have you ever wondered how God can provide for you? We discovered we needed to lay down our own agenda and seek His kingdom first. We began to ask Father God questions. What are You doing? What do You want to do? When we joined in with His plans, His way then provision followed. It was quite a learning experience.

     When we got married, Paul made a good living as a women's apparel sales representative. His territory was Washington, Idaho and Montana. Each new selling season lasted about five to six weeks, with a big push at Market Week held in Seattle and Los Angeles. We had the luxury to live anywhere we wanted as long as Paul could touch base in Seattle.

     We loved boating. We spent our honeymoon cruising in our 26 Reinell Powerboat. Our trip was on the Inside Passage that runs from Washington along the Gulf Islands of British Columbia up to Alaska. Our family spent many good times salmon fishing and collecting mussels and oysters in the protected waters. We spent thrilling hours watching the different pods of Orca Killer Whales frolicking in the water. Friday Harbor-located on San Juan Island in the Strait of Juan de Fuca of Washington State-became a perfect spot to get us closer to the cruising area we so enjoyed. So we decided to give island life a try.

For me, change and leaving my support system-my friends and my church, was scary. As we made the two hour ferry ride, it made me think, *"How much more isolated can we get?"* The car ramp clanged down and our car almost bottomed out as we disembarked the ferry and headed out on the country road that led to Roche Harbor a world famous destination for boaters. During the summer, over six hundred boats would visit daily, but all winter long the marina was empty. Boaters included many famous Hollywood celebrities. John Wayne came every summer. Paul & I were never on his boat, the Gray Goose, but our children were and they made friends with his daughter. We checked out the furnished waterfront condo Paul had found in the newspaper. It looked great even though I was apprehensive because this was a huge change from what I was used to.

Looking out the front window, it reminded me of a painting, it was so gorgeous. Then an eagle landed on the beach right in front of me. *Wow!! Look at the eagle!* I had never seen one so close before! And then a divine whisper calmed my heart.

> *"I carried you on eagle's wings and brought you to myself"* (Ex 19:4). *Thank you Lord,* I silently prayed, *I know you're in this and no matter how different this is going to be, I trust you.*

With no shopping malls, no fast food places, just one traffic light, it was different all right. Before our move, Paul rarely spent an entire evening at home. Now on a twelve-mile long island, where could he go? The answer was… nowhere.

Even home was different now. Frequent power outages explained the large selection of candles the hardware store had to offer and with our five channels of TV gone, we all began to really talk again, and the whole family found time to play games together. We were growing closer to each other and the Lord, everyday. God was really working on both of our hearts. Paul was no longer satisfied with his present walk with the Lord, he wanted more. And God wanted more of Paul, not just Sunday mornings.

Things came to a head when Paul attended some pre-season sales meetings in Minneapolis, MN. Some of the major accounts were getting more discounted merchandise to run better ads and promotions. The smaller store operations were excluded from these discounts. This didn't seem fair to Paul and it affected a lot of his accounts. It became an ethics issue in his heart and Paul felt he couldn't participate any more. He wanted everyone to have the same chance. He told his boss that if the policy didn't change he would leave. This wasn't easy as he was earning about $1000 a week, a very good income for the late seventy's. After building up his nerve to confront them, he did, and was immediately "let go".

Paul had several job offers and went to an interview in the Chicago Merchandise Mart. He found that they all shared that same basic mode of operation, something he wasn't comfortable with any more. He realized he didn't belong in that business any longer. God was shutting a door. *"Now what God,"* Paul prayed. Paul took the elevator down to the Chicago Merchandise Mart lobby. He looked across the lobby and saw a video show in the exhibit hall. Curiosity drew him to see the new technology developments. Paul had previously pursued a career in photography while in high school and television production in his college days. What he saw was a new world. There had been so many advances over the years. Video production was just being introduced. It took Paul several hours just to see all that was now available. When he finally left the arena, Paul heard God say, *"I want you to use this new technology to spread the gospel."*

    Back at home, I had been fasting with a sense that God wanted my obedience in this action. This was completely new to me, missing a meal seemed pretty extreme. I didn't know what was happening to Paul, but I knew something pivotal was unfolding. *"Lord, I need Your help to obey You in this."* For me, that was the beginning of learning to lean on Him, not to trust in my own strength and to follow Him. I was surprised as I prepared meals for my children; I really wasn't hungry, not really even tempted. I kept my normal routine of jogging and taking care of the house and kids. I added more praise music and less TV, more prayer, less conversation. I'm chatty, but I needed to guard that sense of serenity and peace. I was less connected to the natural world and more engaged with the Lord in my spirit man. My appetite didn't return until that Monday when Paul got back home. We walked the docks at Roche Harbor and Paul told me about hearing God's call. We joined our hands and hearts saying *"Yes Lord,"* leaving us grateful, excited, awestruck and a little scared.

    We planned to live on the checks from the previous season, and then we maxed out our credit card. We were trying to live by faith, but if God didn't come through, we still had our own cushion to fall back on. Now that cushion was getting smaller and smaller. We really didn't have a practical model to go by. Paul and I took a whole day to really "hear" God. We came away assured we needed to do whatever it took to step into the video world and spread the gospel. We prayed, and putting everything we had on the altar, we said, *"Lord, if you want us to keep this boat, please provide the payment."* Nothing came in so the boat was gone. We did the same thing with our car, gone. We joked, *"Everything we put on the altar goes right out the door."*

During the summer, a dear brother in the Lord from Seattle leant us an extra car he had, a VW convertible. Good thing I knew how to drive a stick. But I guess God knew that. The owners of an even more deluxe 3 bedroom penthouse condo asked us to live in their unit to prevent water damage like they'd suffered the previous winter. We paid a ridiculous low rent of $350 a month and they used it one month in the summer. Thank you Lord! After three years we moved out and it was sold for nearly $1,000,000.

How do you actually seek God's kingdom first? In the beginning, Paul was asked to give his testimony at various men's meetings about using the media to spread the gospel. One time he called after speaking at FGBMFI in Vancouver, B.C. He was working to obtain a TV station license for the Christian channel, 24. None existed at that time and channel 24 would cover Seattle and Vancouver. I told him we were broke and he needed to come home to seek God for our needs. When he returned we took our Bibles and some Hagen tapes to the beach. It was deserted and there were miles of beach in each direction. We found a big log for a back rest and settled in for a day of prayer, study and listening. The outcome was the verse from

> *Matt. 6:33   Seek the Kingdom of God above all else, and live righteously, and he will give you everything you need. (NLT)*

Paul stopped running around speaking and started seeking "HIM" first. Within a week, things began to change.

We decided one way to seek first the kingdom of God in our own community was by encouraging new life in the Holy Spirit. We wanted to help build up the established church and bring unity through inter-denominational groups. I was one of a few women involved in prayer meetings asking God how to begin. Our answer came when a gal moved to the island that had been active in Women's Aglow in Oregon. With a few months of prayer and growing together, a board was raised up and a Friday Harbor Aglow was launched, as well as a Full Gospel Businessman's Fellowship a few months later.

One speaker for the FGBMF told us we needed to be asking God for our daily bread. I looked in the cupboards and we had some cereal and noodles and bread. I said *"God, I really don't need more bread for dinner, we need something to go with all these noodles, I'm trying to trust you, but I don't know how."* Then my son Lloyd, in third grade at the time, came bursting through the door, sounding real excited. *"Mom, look what I got!"* I couldn't believe my eyes. He was holding a nice sized salmon. He said, *"I felt like walking home along the beach instead of taking the road and this eagle flew over and dropped this salmon right in front of me. I made a run for it and I got it. Pretty cool, huh?"* *"Very cool, very good, very God,"* I said. The same God who used ravens to feed Elijah (1 Kings 17:4), caused my son to choose a different way home so an eagle could drop a salmon right where he could get it. We really said extraordinary thanks over that meal. It's still the best salmon dinner I've ever had.

So we were started on God's economy. There was always enough. There were so many acts of God's faithfulness to us, it's hard to know what to include here.

We lived in a deluxe condo as I said, and once while Paul and I were away in Washington, D.C. concerning a TV station, someone left three bags of groceries on our back step full of the special treats our children loved. We had stocked up the pantry before we left with necessities, but these bags were full of their favorites. Their grandma thought the store had made a special delivery. It was special all right, delivered by God. But I often wonder about the outrageous obedience it took to leave groceries on the steps of a million dollar condo. We never did find out who left them.

The month we needed to move out, a Christian brother leant us his Airstream travel trailer. We stayed at Lonesome Cove, a local waterfront camp ground. This cove was used to film "Namu." The weather was so great we served most of our meals outside on the picnic table. We really enjoyed the whole experience and got such great sun tans, a false rumor circulated that we'd vacationed in Hawaii on ministry funds. Our lessons in forgiving began.

We were leaning on the promise, God will supply all your needs (Phil 4:19), but sometimes we just had a "want," not really a need. One time Lloyd had been craving a Coke. We didn't have enough money to buy soda, but we prayed, asking God to bring him a coke somehow. We had this big condo, so we held potluck praise gatherings at our home. That night when everyone picked up their dishes and left, there was a single bottle of Coke sitting on the counter labeled, "for Lloyd," *Thank you Lord*. It was the real thing!

Another time, our daughter Susan and I were grocery shopping and she wanted apple juice. Again, I didn't have enough money and I felt especially bad since Susan often felt left out as a second child. *"I'm sorry, honey, I just don't have enough for that. Let's ask God to provide."* She had a defeated shrug that said, it figures. *"How's he going to do that? Send apple juice from the sky." "I don't know," I said,* as I put my arm around her. *"Let's just try."* So I prayed and as we walked down each aisle, I kept waiting for something to happen, but nothing did. We got in line at the checkout counter, still no juice from heaven. Then one of my friends from prayer group came up behind me and said, *"I'm so glad I ran into you, I keep forgetting,"* she rummaged in her purse; *"here's the five dollars you leant me."* She put the bill in my hand. *"Thanks for helping me out."* I still don't remember lending it to her, but inside I did a little happy, thank you Jesus dance. *"Apple juice"* I sang out waving the bill above my head, Susan had a huge grin as she went to get the juice God had provided for her.

Looking back, it doesn't make sense. We'd meet the right people we needed to, just when we were ready to take the next step. We'd see a need and ask God how we could fill it. Our own teens needed a camp to help build them up, so we organized a retreat for teens on the island. The ministry team consisted of friends that already had a heart for youth. Many teens gave their hearts to Jesus which started a revival that swept generations into the kingdom. God had a mighty plan for the families on that tiny island and we had a part in it. It was amazing! That teen camp birthed a family camp the following year. There we met some terrific speakers and that led to accompanying them on trips to Israel for intercession and teaching, along with Holy Land Tours. Ministry Trips to Israel led to a FGBMFI trip to Ireland, then several trips to Japan and then Taiwan where many were healed, saved and filled with the Holy Spirit.

These trips led to our relationship with Charles and Francis Hunter to facilitate their "Healing Explosions" in Japan, Taiwan, the Philippines and eventually China. That led to us taking healing teams for Healing Explosions into Germany, Holland, France, England, Denmark and many other nations. Our personal friendships in God's family opened the doors.

There were challenging times as well as times of testing. During this season of learning to forgive, there was one occasion where I felt betrayed by a close friend. I was right and they were definitely wrong. I heard God say, *"Go and ask for their forgiveness" "No way!"* I stubbornly refused. They needed to come to me. I was not going to make the first move. For two days, I was miserable. I felt like I was wrestling with God. The pressure of my own bitterness and disobedience weighed me down. Finally, I gave in. Paul and I went together. We apologized and forgiveness restored God's peace to each of us as we all released our pain and disappointments. That day God said, *"Now I can open a door for you Paul and Lynn to the nations."*

We had everything we needed. We never went hungry, although sometimes we did eat a lot of macaroni and cheese. One time we moved into a house that both of us thought was fully furnished. When we got to the house with our first load on moving day, there was no furniture at all! They thought we were talking about the appliances. *"Did we miss You God?"* We sensed a peace. No mistake, this was our new home, I guess it showed we were growing in faith. That night, we all slept in the living room on the mint green carpeting. We were helping with a Charismatic prayer group in Seattle the following Friday and we shared with them how we'd accidently moved into an unfurnished house. One of the couples said, *"You can use the furniture from our lake house, we won't be using it until next summer."* We were very grateful, *the Lord HAD provided*. When the truck arrived we couldn't believe our eyes. There was an entire house full of furniture. The first thing off the truck was a mint green sofa and chairs that matched the carpet perfectly! The master bedroom set seemed as if it had been made for that room. It fit perfectly even though the closet and windows had an awkward placement. There was a complete bedroom set for both Lloyd and Susan, and a dinette set with four chairs that fit right in our small breakfast nook. Praise God!! Martha Stewart couldn't have done better!!

There was a time Paul's travel demands increased; he sensed he should get his pilot's license. Ground school was affordable so we started there. Then provision came in for flying lessons, and for the plane that was leased, a Cessna 172. Paul saw the plane in a newspaper ad and called the owner. He told the owner we were in ministry and our Island location made travel time too consuming, five hours to Seattle each way. The owner told him he was praying for the plane to be used for spreading the Gospel. He leased us the plane for $200 per month and it served us for nearly four years.

Then our car died and for a couple months, we had an airplane but no car. We took turns riding on the back of Lloyd's Kawasaki dirt bike the half-mile to the airfield. We flew from Roche Harbor to Friday Harbor for groceries and even flew to Victoria, B.C. for church. God's ways aren't our ways (Is. 55:8), but our transportation needs were met.

Our ministry has taken us overseas over one hundred times, to many nations. We have operated as an independent ministry, not because we wanted to, but because no ministry wanted to take a risk on us. No church or ministry has ever directly supported us. Ministries we assisted sometimes provided expenses and some support. Individuals have heard God and provided, many times sacrificially.

Paul details the first $5000 check we received in another chapter. A woman visiting from California came up to us at the Lonesome Cove Resort and gave us $7,000. She had been recently married and this was all of her personal money. For 2 years, a Catholic family supported our work with the youth. Every month Paul would meet with the benefactor of the Catholic family and show him our ministry budget for the next month. He would write us a check without questions.

Our nation and the world are facing difficult times. Recently, Paul attended a seminar with speakers such as Rudy Giuliani, General Colin Powell and Zig Ziglar. They all talked about the financial dilemmas in our nation and around the world; energy costs, inflation, jobs and uncertainty. When Paul got home from the seminar he was praising God, *"We are on God's financial plan."*

The Power of Agreement

Lynn Crawford

In one of the shadow times of my life, God gave me a valuable revelation that led me out of the pit I was in. To this day, it continues to liberate me and everyone I share it with.

I had been fighting chronic sinus infections for months. Antibiotics were no longer effective; I'd taken so many of them for way too long. I know it doesn't sound like much, but the exhaustion and constant headaches were robbing me of a normal life. Since I was barely able to get off the couch, let alone go to the park with my son, an energetic preschooler; we hired a young Christian woman to help. She was truly an answer to my prayers.

But as if a sinus infection wasn't bad enough, I was also diagnosed clinically depressed. I suffered deep shame because I was taking anti-depressants. All of me; my mind, my body and my emotions were under attack...I had no reserves...no energy and no hope. By this time, I had been a Christian for years; I was also singing and leading worship-which had always been a big part of my walk with the Lord. Now I was battling to make peace with my grief, my depression, and God as I knew Him.

During this season, God was still using me by allowing me to speak into people's lives at women's groups. Many times I'd be too weak to drive myself anywhere, but as I led worship the strength I needed would come. I would also share what I was learning about forgiveness and I would pray for people. When I did, there was always good fruit of the Holy Spirit, especially healing. Ironically, there were several confirmed healings of depression, even though I went home still needing medication.

One day I reached my breaking point. Desperately, I cried out *"God, I can't take this anymore. I want to be whole. But I don't know how. The spiritual warfare techniques I've studied are way over my head. I just don't get it. Teach me how to win this Lord. But please, God, make it simple, like warfare for dummies, something even I can do."*

I was reading the gospel of John that day and when I got to Chapter 14 verse 30-I knew… Ta-da! This is what I've been looking for. For the next two hours, the Holy Spirit was my Teacher on spiritual warfare, personally tutoring me

> In John 14:30, Jesus says *"I won't talk with you much more for the prince (evil genius, ruler) of this world is coming and he has no claim on Me. He has nothing in common with ME, there is nothing in ME that belong to him, and he has no power over Me"* (Amp)

As the Holy Spirit began to search me and do an interior "inventory", I knew I couldn't say the same. I did have things in common with the enemy of my soul.

Did Satan have a claim on me? No, I've been bought by the Blood of Jesus. He has no claim on me. But If Satan can convince me to add to the Cross, trust in my own efforts or goodness along with the Cross, I've left myself open to his attacks of condemnation and more. Was there any mixture of false teaching? *"You don't need a Savior. You are a god over yourself. There is no sin; there is no heaven or hell, only what you create."*

Satan hates Jesus, our Savior, the Cross and especially the Blood. That's where he suffered his eternal defeat.

> *Col. 2:13-15 When you were dead in your sins and in the uncircumcision of your sinful nature, God made you alive with Christ. He forgave us all our sins, having canceled the written code, with its regulations, that was against us and that stood opposed to us; He took it away, nailing it to the Cross. And having DISARMED the powers and authorities, He made a public spectacle of them, triumphing over them by the Cross.* (NIV)

Do Satan and I have anything in common? Do we share any common beliefs, attitudes and behaviors? Regrettably, I had to answer…yes. He starts with our mind insinuating, *"There's no real harm in this sin, just once won't hurt,"* and if we don't resist, it leads to action.

When we are tired or weakened in our own personal wilderness, one of Satan's favorite tactics is to plant doubt within us about God's Word and His promises to us, *"Has God really said?"*

Under this pressure, I did fall into doubts..."*maybe God isn't going to heal me, maybe this is as good as I'm going to get"* and many more. I was convicted, so out loud I confessed,

"Forgive me Lord for agreeing with Satan and doubting You and Your Word." A scripture came into my mind, *"I've entered a 'covenant of Peace (wholeness, nothing lacking) with you and it will not depart from you."*

> Isa. 54:10   *"For the mountains may move and the hills disappear, but even then my faithful love for you will remain. My covenant of blessing will never be broken," says the Lord, who has mercy on you.* NLT

More and more scriptures came to my mind, and as I prayed them out loud, my anxiety faded away. *"You sent Your Word and healed me. (Ps.107:20) "By your stripes I am healed"* (Is. 53:4&5)

It's no wonder Satan tries to get us to doubt God's Word. Jesus showed us that God's Word is an effective weapon as He responded to the enemy in His wilderness battle. Jesus countered every doubting arrow flung at Him with, *IT IS WRITTEN. (Matt. 4:1-11)* Now I keep a small notebook filled with scriptures that have encouraged me or given me strength in the past-my own personal arsenal to resist the enemy. I can manage my inner dialogue to line up with God's Word. *"Today, I am one day closer to my total healing in Jesus Name."*

Satan is a liar and the father of lies, (Jn 8:44) He's also called the accuser of the brethren, that's you and every one that loves Jesus, your pastor, your church, any believer. He attacks God's character and God's children. He will "tell" you God doesn't love you anymore because…*you're divorced, you've had an abortion, you're struggling with sin or addiction, you keep blowing it, yelling at your kids, falling off your diet, you've committed the unpardonable sin*…all his lies are old stuff, but effective. Either *"you're dirt"* or *"you're too good for these losers." "nobody likes you at this church don't go any more, this church is full of hypocrites, your faith is so superior, don't go getting infected by these wimps."*

When the Holy Spirit convicts you of sin, He's specific-but loving. *"Don't say that, don't do that, don't go there, apologize for that, make peace with that person,"* whereas the enemy slings condemnation at you which is a general feeling of, *"you're just terrible."* What's wonderful is that as soon as we come out of agreement with satan, we're in agreement with God. And that's the best!! When the Holy Spirit is in control, we see the evidence. Like apples on an apple tree. The fruit of the Holy Spirit is love, joy, peace, patience, kindness, goodness, faithfulness, gentleness, and self-control. (Gal. 6:22) The fruit is there because the Holy Spirit is present and BEING Himself.

Just the opposites are the arrows that the enemy aims at our "flesh". Hate, unforgiveness, depression, anxiety instead of praying and trusting, do it yourself right now instead of being patient, hard hearted, evil, unfaithful, harsh, out of control. If our fleshy attitudes aren't lassoed and made obedient to Christ, they can trip us up. (2 Cor. 10:3-5) Galatians 6:19 lists the acts of the flesh and says they're obvious.

> *Gal. 5:19   When you follow the desires of your sinful nature, the results are very clear: sexual immorality, impurity, lustful pleasures, 20 idolatry, sorcery, hostility, quarreling, jealousy, outbursts of anger, selfish ambition, dissension, division, 21 envy, drunkenness, wild parties, and other sins like these. Let me tell you again, as I have before, that anyone living that sort of life will not inherit the Kingdom of God. NLT*

Some Bible translations call them works. Just like you have to get up, get dressed, and get to work, it takes effort. These things don't just happen, you have to choose, and then DO. Sexual immorality, impurity, debauchery, idolatry and witchcraft; hatred, discord, jealousy, fits of rage, selfish ambition, dissensions, factions and envy; drunkenness, orgies and the like. These "fleshly things" tear away at our relationships with God and others.

Paul warns that if we live like this, we won't inherit the benefits of the Kingdom of God, nor will we be able to enjoy them in our everyday life. As with the fruit of the Holy Spirit, Jesus said,

> *John 10:10 The thief's purpose is to steal and kill and destroy. My purpose is to give them a rich and satisfying life. NLT Plenty of love, plenty of peace and joy sounds good to me.*

Don't excuse your flesh with words like, *"I'm hot tempered, I'm Italian, I was tired, if you wouldn't do that I wouldn't get mad."* Now that we're born again, we're called to get rid of that old stuff (Eph. 4:30-31). Jesus will help us do anything He commands us to do. Anger, fear and unforgiveness can rob us of that abundant life.

> **Anger:** (Eph. 4:26) a*nd don't sin by letting anger control you. Don't let the sun go down while you are still angry, 27 for anger gives a foothold to the devil.*

This can be tough to walk out. When Paul and I tried to talk things out late at night, it just got worse. We were too tired, we had short fuses and it just seemed to make things worse. What works for us-which took us twenty-five years to discover-is we try to not get into anything dicey after 9pm. If we do, we make the decision to give our conflict to the Lord for now. In the morning, or after work, we will respectfully listen to each other and resolve it then. So I have to not seethe or keep rehashing everything but table it until later. I'm personally convinced that anger and unforgiveness releases toxins in our body that cause all kinds of problems-depression and joint pain for example. Going to sleep angry may be flooding your system with an overnight toxic infusion.

> **Fear:** The "what ifs" fear throws at you can really shut you down. Fear of rejection, afraid to speak, afraid to pray for someone, fear of what if nothing happens?

Fear comes from believing in a negative outcome. Faith believes that God will bring something good out of it all.

1 Jn. 4:18   there is no fear in love. But perfect love drives out fear.

Our God IS perfect love…so do step out in loving faith and trust the results to God. We are all just learning and no one is perfect. Pick up that phone and tell your friend that she was on your heart, and then say those loving words that God gave you for her. Maybe she'll show how much it meant; maybe she'll say, *"I'm fine, why did you call?"* You can just say, *"I had a nudge I thought was from God–I'm learning."* The best scenario is when she knows that you and God both care about her. That's a good thing.

> **Forgiveness**: Our God forgives and forgets.
> *Jer.31:34   "And I will forgive their wickedness, and I will never again remember their sins."*

We need to forgive, forgive and forgive some more. We're all human and we hurt each other unintentionally and on purpose. The enemy will try to convince you that you have a just reason not to forgive. Then he has you locked in that pain. Forgiving is a decision to be obedient, and letting go of your right to punish the one who hurt you; not because they are innocent, but because of all that Jesus did for us on the Cross. He paid the full price for every sin we've committed and everything that was ever done against us, so we can confidently pray out loud, *"Jesus, I choose to forgive anyone who hurt me…I entrust them to You to deal with. I can't really forget, Lord, but whenever they come to my mind I will bless them, praying Your best for them. Thank you God that today I am free of the sin of unforgiveness."*

> **Bless those who persecute you:** *Bless and do not curse. Pray for those who mistreat you (Ro. 12:14 & Luke 6:28).*

Satan doesn't want you free, so they will probably come to your mind again and again, but keep on declaring that you've forgiven them and bless them-silently and out loud. Out loud is best when you are able. Make an extra trip to the bathroom for the privacy if needed.

The last category on my inner search of *"nothing in me that belongs to him"* was whether or not I owned any objects devoted to Satan and the occult.

> **Idols/Occult:** Deut 7:25   *"You must burn their idols in fire, and you must not covet the silver or gold that covers them. You must not take it or it will become a trap to you, for it is detestable to the Lord your God. 26 Do not bring any detestable objects into your home, for then you will be destroyed, just like them. You must utterly detest such things, for they are set apart for destruction." NLT*

I learned this truth early in our walk with the Lord. We rented a completely furnished condo with a beautiful water view. It was decorated with a pretty Buddha and an expensive painting depicting some form of idol worship. After we moved in, there was a marked increase of conflict between Paul and me. Even our children were at it with each other. It went beyond "normal." Even my women's prayer group that met at my house seemed different. They were not as open to the Holy Spirit and people weren't receiving the baptism in the Holy Spirit like before. Something was wrong. I prayed about it. Asking God to show me what it was; I sensed *"You need to anoint the house and dedicate it to the Lord."* I wanted Paul to join me (unity, two or more, all that kind of stuff); looking back, I wanted to pass the assignment God had given me to Paul. This even turned out to be a minor skirmish, but I got some cooking oil and Paul met me at the front door with a belligerent, *"Now what?"* We'd never done this before, but I remembered the Passover in Exodus 12, and how it talked about the anointing of the doorposts with blood from the lamb; so I figured we could do something like that and start with our door. So Paul took the oil and made a sign of the Cross above the door praying, *"Lord we dedicate this home to You, Satan has no place here, we pray no evil enters through this door, Jesus, You alone are Lord here."* Immediately, we both sensed a change in the atmosphere...the frustration was gone and a heavy sense of God's peaceful presence surrounded us. *"Whoa, I think we're on to something,"* I said. We went into each and every room; anointing and praying as we felt led for God's best to reign in our home. When we got to the room with the Buddha, unrest crept back into our spirits. The Buddha represented a false religion that keeps millions from the One True God. It didn't belong in our home. We confessed, *"Lord, now we see this object doesn't please you, so it's out of here. Show us anything else you don't want in our home."* There was more. My Egyptian Nephritides 14 ct. gold necklace Paul bought me in Egypt was sentimental and valuable. But Deut. 7: 25 warned against coveting the gold, so it had to go. There were some posters and music and of course, the expensive painting. The things that belonged to us, we could dispose of. But the things that belonged to our landlord, that was different. We decided to put most of his stuff in a separate storage area away from our home. We couldn't afford for the painting to get damaged so we both prayed and agreed to cover it with a sheet and hang a cross on it.

The whole atmosphere in our home changed, we were having fun together instead of arguing. At our next prayer meeting, my friend received the baptism in the Holy Spirit with her very own prayer language. There were healings and words of encouragement, the gifts of the Holy Spirit (1 Cor. 12) were poured out on us that day. Praise God! It was a dramatic change and made such a big difference in our life, so we included *"Freedom from Accursed Things"* in our seminar GOD'S HEALING POWER THROUGH YOU.

We taught our seminar at Pastor Peter Wenz's church in Stuttgart, Germany. Their love for one another and openness to the Holy Spirit caused them to rapidly outgrow their church that held only 300 people; they had to rent a hall that would seat 2,000. It was packed for our teaching, with another 200 downstairs in an overflow room watching everything on live video. As usual, we included *Power of Agreement* and *Freedom from Accursed Things*. We saw many dramatic healings, and hundreds set free that weekend.

Six years later, Paul was in Stuttgart videotaping another Christian conference when a woman approached him smiling. *"I want to give you this"* she said, pressing 1000 Marks into Paul's hand. *"I'm so happy to see you again. Your teaching saved my life! I attended the seminar you held here six years ago. We were having big problems, one health crisis after another. That caused our finances to suffer since we were unable to work. In addition, we had serious troubles with our children; illnesses and addictions. The mental and physical pressure was unbearable. When we heard your teaching on accursed things, we immediately went home and with the Holy Spirit we had a spiritual house cleaning. We got rid of many things and had a nudge that we should include our expensive hand woven rug from Iran. But it was very valuable and beautiful and I didn't want to let it go. Still we still didn't have the release we were expecting. When I prayed, I would hear "Look at the rug. Look more closely at the rug" so I contacted an expert to come look at it. He told me it was exquisite, especially the prayers hand woven throughout the entire rug. That was enough for me...we destroyed it that very night. The turnaround was immediate. Our health, finances and relationships were totally restored. We can't thank you enough and we just want to bless you and your ministry."*

When we were in China, our guide gave our son Joel, who was four at the time, a miniature temple to remember our tour. I was battling some strange physical problems that just wouldn't go away. When we got to Japan, Joel showed our missionary friends his souvenir. She then told me privately that enemy spirits can attach themselves to that type of object that symbolizes a false religion and interfere with our receiving all God has for us. Joel gave it to her and she took him shopping for a toy of his choice. She disposed of it and I began to get better right away.

When we were teaching in Manila, Joel walked all the way up to the platform in front of every one and said, "Don't forget to tell them to get rid of any god houses they have".

We've seen many set free when they removed accursed items from their homes. I want to encourage you to prayerfully go through your own possessions asking the Lord if there's anything that doesn't belong in your home. Buddha's, temples, tiki gods, religious masks, occult objects, idol worship, ancestor worship, Egyptian or new age. This is incomplete, but if you ask the Holy Spirit, He will show you if there's something that is attracting enemy attention to you. Involvements with horoscopes, séances, fortune telling, New Age, spirit guides, channelers and Ouija boards, are forbidden and can provide an opening for evil.

> *Deut. 18:10   Let no one be found among you who sacrifices his son or daughter in the fire, who practices divination or sorcery, interprets omens, engages in witchcraft or casts spells, or who is a medium or spiritist or who consults the dead. Anyone who does these things is detestable to the Lord because these practices are detestable.*

If you've participated in any of these things you can be totally free by confessing your sin, promising never to do it again and letting the blood of Jesus wash you totally clean. (Gal. 3:13 NLT) Christ has rescued us from the curse pronounced by the law when He was hung on the Cross; He took upon Himself the curse for our wrong doing. The blessing God gives extends to a thousand generations. (Psalm 105:8)

Thank God! We can be healed now. This is a process much like restoring furniture; removing layer after layer of gunk, and learning a better way of living and loving and walking with Jesus. I think 1 John1:7 says it best-*If we walk in the light, as He is in the light, we have fellowship with one another, and the blood of Jesus, His Son, purifies us from all sin.* We can have that today. It's just one aspect of the wonderful abundant life Jesus wants us to have.

Franco Set Free

Lynn Crawford

We eventually moved to Bellevue, WA from San Juan Island, at which time I was feeling very alone. During a Healing Explosion Ministry Team trip in Manila, Philippines, I suffered an ectopic pregnancy, which is where the embryo starts growing in the fallopian tube and the fallopian tube bursts, causing an infection in the abdomen. After seeing hundreds of healings, to be hospitalized in a life threatening situation was surreal. God held me so close in that hospital. I talk about this in detail, in the chapter, *Healing Place*. He answered my prayer and I was able to return home early and be with my children for a short time. We went ahead with our scheduled move even though I couldn't lift or do much while still recovering from the surgery.

Lloyd and Susan being older teenagers at the time chose to remain in Friday Harbor. Compounded with losing the baby and other personal losses, this was just too much for me. The loneliness and depression swamped me. Now we were settled in a fast paced city, a bedroom community of Seattle, so it was harder to connect. I met a couple mothers through Joel's preschool friends but it would take time to build meaningful relationships, friends like I'd had at Friday Harbor are rare. Paul was very involved in ministry trips with the FGBMFI, and I was masking a lot of my sadness so he didn't realize how depressed I really was. But in spite of counseling, medication and prayer, I was sinking. It seemed everything would go wrong whenever Paul left on a trip. The car would break down, Joel or I would get sick, problems, problems, problems.

I wanted to throw a pity party so I called a mentor of mine who had served as a missionary in Brazil and raised her family there. *"Why does everything always happen to me?"* I barely started whining when she stopped me cold. *"Quit broadcasting how the devil can beat you up. You're telling him how to keep you down. Don't give up and crawl in a hole. Fight! Resist! Start believing God not your feelings. Believe His promises and speak His Word into your situation. Stop your whining and FIGHT!!"*

The truth hurt, but at least she loved me enough to shake me out of my negativity. I had to say, *"You're right. Thanks God. I needed that."* The truth will set you free if it doesn't kill you first. This habit of my flesh really did need to die if my life was going to change for the better. I hung up the phone and went straight to the Throne. I made a quality decision to change, stop hiding and start acting in faith. Immediately, I prayed out loud, *"Lord, forgive me for being passive and forfeiting many of my spiritual battles. I'm not going to pull the covers over my head and hide away with a Snicker Bars any more. I will take action, I will resist the Devil and from now on, I will fight."* There were no bolts of lightening but I knew I'd done business with God and now, putting on the spiritual armor God gave us, especially His belt of truth, would be an important part of my daily routine.

I began to deal with my emotions in a new way instead of hiding or masking them. I was learning to bring each one into God's light and resolve my hurt and disappointments one at a time, in His loving Word. I realized the power I'd handed the enemy to rob me when these old hurts were shoved down and denied instead of dealt with God's way.

Several weeks later, I was back in Manila with Charles and Francis Hunter and their healing ministry teams. I had renewed passion to bring healing to the broken hearted and let the oppressed go free. *(Is. 61:1and Luke 4:18)*

> *Luke 4:18-19 "The Spirit of the LORD is upon me, for he has anointed me to bring Good News to the poor. He has sent me to proclaim that captives will be released, that the blind will see, that the oppressed will be set free, 19 and that the time of the LORD's favor has come." NLT*

We held the meeting at an outdoor stadium to facilitate the larger crowd. After a much anointed praise and worship time, I started to take my seat at the far end of the raised stage. A woman on the floor got my attention and beckoned me to come to her. She met me at the bottom of the stairs and took my hand, imploring me to come and pray for her brother. She told me he had a demon that gave him such super human strength he'd actually lifted a refrigerator all by himself and thrown it. All their friends and family were terrified. I agreed to go and looked for Paul but he had his hands full so I asked one of the pastors in our group to come with us. I think it's always better to minister in twos and especially in this kind of situation. She led us through the crowd to her brother. He was rolling around in the dirt and loudly snarling and crying. A large circle of people had formed a safe distance around him, I think they were watching and praying. The circle opened up for us to approach him as I was secretly praying an S.O.S. HELP, prayer. *"O my God, God help! I am way over my* head here, Jesus. This is way too much for me." I was relieved I had the pastor with me to handle this, so I turned to ask him what he wanted to do first and he wasn't behind me. He was back in the circle and gestured for me to go for it. Beneath that part of me that was scared to death, I could sense God's peace. That comforted me some and then His still small voice directed me. *"Don't be afraid. I want to use you in this. I will guide you every step of the way. Perfect love casts out fear (1 John 4:18). I love you. Just trust me."* "Okay, Lord." I was still anxious, but at least willing. *"Let's do this".* By then, someone had helped him to his feet. He was quite a sight. As bad as he looked, filthy hair, torn clothing, dirt everywhere, it was his foaming at the mouth that really got to me. I was definitely getting queasy. Now he was standing close to me, way too close. And this thought shot into my head, *"He's going to spit on you."* I looked at that foam dripping down his chin and his yellowed teeth and I thought, *"If he spits on me, I'll just shrivel up and die."* I wanted out of there or at least back away so I was out of spitting range. *"Don't step back. Stand still."* The Holy Spirit warned me. Then I remembered the verse, *I have given you power and authority over all the power of the enemy-you can walk among snakes and scorpions and nothing will injure you, Luke 10:19 NLT.* The Amplified version says and nothing shall in any way harm you. Looking him right in the eye, I prayed out loud, *"I thank You Lord for the Cross. I thank you I'm completely covered by Your Blood, Jesus. I know, Lord, You absolutely defeated Satan at the Cross stripped him of all his power. Then you gave me, Your very Own Child, authority over all the works of the enemy. You promised that nothing would by any means harm me. Getting spit on would be harmful to me, Lord, so I'm grateful that that's not going to happen. I bind you, you evil spirit, from spitting or harming me in any way in the Name of Jesus."* Then that spirit spoke in a creepy voice, *"I know you. You are a fighter."* It had a tone of awe in it, which is completely yucky to think about a devil complimenting you, and I'm sure it was just meant to make me get into a pride thing and thinking "Yes. I'm all that!" Now, I know to bind the spirits and not allow them to speak at all because they are such liars.

In my mind, I saw myself that day of decision in my kitchen. I realized that this enemy spirit knew about that day when I repented and decided to fight. He knew what I had said out loud. I don't think the enemy can read our minds, but he does insert thoughts into our minds that we need to resist. That's why we have to bring every thought captive and in agreement with God's Word and the Cross. (2 Cor. 10:5) I thank God our past hurts and sins are all under the Blood and He has His own timetable for restoring our souls. Satan has no access to them. But when God shines His light on something that's hindering us, usually asking us to forgive or repent, if we refuse, then that act of rebellion can open us up to an attack.

"Be quiet, you devil. You are a liar just like your father, Satan. Only Jesus matters. I'm here in His Name, in His strength to enforce the total victory He won at the Cross." Then I looked directly at the man and asked him his name. *"Franco,"* he said quietly. *"Do you want to be free of this spirit, Franco?"* he didn't answer, his sister told me that he'd gone to a witch doctor to get this spirit and it's powers. Meanwhile, the Holy Spirit was letting me know that he had all kinds of stuff in his possession that was accursed and that this spirit was attached to. *"Don't command it to go until those things are removed,"* the Holy Spirit impressed on me. I knew his family wanted him delivered, but I wasn't so sure he wanted to give up these powers. *"Franco, I told him, if you want to be friends with Jesus and be set free, you have to get rid of all that occult stuff you have and you have to be willing to break off your relationship with this spirit that empowers you."* I saw a small room in my imagination, with a wooden bookshelf, so I

began to name the specific occult objects displayed there. *"You have books, candles, some pictures, there's a necklace and some rings."* Whenever I named something, he would nod yes, *"all your occult stuff has to go if you want Jesus to set you free."* Then I turned to his sister, *"I can't lay hands on him unless he really wants to be free, he has to get rid of everything that's connected to the occult. If he does that, bring him back here tomorrow and we can pray for him."* His sister agreed and thanking me, she gave me a hug. We were all encouraged that God was doing something because God had shown me his room and all that stuff. The gifts the Holy Spirit gives really do build up our trust and faith. (1 Cor. 12:1-11).

    The next morning was Sunday so we went to our friends' church service there in Manila. He and his wife were going to be part of the healing service that afternoon. I told her about Franco. She said she'd be glad to partner with me if he came back. They had dealt with this kind of stuff before and she wasn't intimidated. We all had a great time with the Lord and there were several instant back healings where the pain left completely. We all went to the sports field excited to see what all God would do. The praise and worship was very enthusiastic and LOUD!! I saw some movement by a huge bank of speakers and there was Franco and his sister. She was smiling and waving at me, happy to be back. I motioned my friend and nodded in their direction and so she followed me down the stairs to join them. His sister assured us he had burned all his occult objects and wanted to be free. We could barely hear her or even think the music was so loud; we were right in front of those mammoth speakers. The evil spirit threw Franco to the ground and he was thrashing about something terrible. The Holy Spirit told me, *"Command the spirit to get up and walk with you to a quieter place."* I didn't know I could do that, but I repeated the command, *"Spirit, I command you in the*

Name of Jesus to get up and walk with us to a quieter place." Franco got up, my friend and I took his elbows and walked with him between us. At the edge of the crowd, the spirit lifted him up and he did a 360 degree somersault in mid air and came back down in front of us. *"This looks good to me."* My friend agreed. I took a good look at Franco. His eyes didn't even look human; they looked more like an angry wolf ready to pounce on me. *"What now? Lord"* I asked. *"Tell him I love him. Tell him I will never hurt him like his father did."* *"Jesus loves you, Franco"*, I began. *"He would never hurt you like your father did. He paid the price for your sins by shedding His own Blood on the Cross. He came to save you."* He began to weep and I embraced him as he sobbed on my shoulder. I shared the Gospel with Franco, he cried even more. We were in the beautiful presence of Jesus. My friend and his sister began softly singing Jesus Loves Me. *"Do you accept Jesus as your personal Savior, Franco?"* *"Yes,"* he replied. *"Do you forgive your father? He just didn't know any better."* *"Yes."* God's love was pouring over him and I could feel him relax all over. *"Do you renounce Satan and all his works?"* *"Yes."* Then break off your relationship with this foul spirit and tell him to go. *"Leave me,"* Franco said firmly, *"I don't want you. I just want Jesus."* *"In Jesus Name,"* I declared, *"I bind you devil, and I command you to go and never return."* God's peace came over all of us. Then Franco repeated the sinner's prayer after me and when he said Amen he was a new creation. (2 Cor. 5:17-21 NLB) What this means is that those who become Christians become new persons. They are not the same any more, for the old life is gone. A new life has begun! All this newness of life is from God who brought us back to Himself through what Christ did. And God has given us the task of reconciling people to Him. *For God was in Christ, reconciling the world to Himself, no longer counting people's sins against them. This is the wonderful message he has given us to tell others. We are Christ's ambassadors, and God is using us to speak to you. We urge you, as though Christ Himself were here pleading with you, be reconciled to God! For God made, Christ, who never sinned, to be an offering for our sin, so that we could be made right with God through Christ.* Franco smiled; his eyes were soft and full of life. He looked like a completely different man. We all hugged him and cried with joy. My friend took him under her wing and invited him to their church to be discipled. It was the most gentle, beautiful miracle I'd ever seen.

A couple of years later, when we saw our pastor friends, she told me Franco had grown so fast in the Lord and that he led his entire family including his father to Jesus. And he was leading a neighborhood Bible Study where several had received Jesus. I learned later that he went on to Bible College and is now a pastor in Manila.

That nasty spirit got access through the abuse Franco had suffered as a small child; offering him power when Franco really needed Jesus. The manifestations were meant to scare us away. It all turned out to be one of the easiest but most dramatic transformations I've ever seen. We all need to look past the manifestations, and let the Holy Spirit reveal to us the real person; the one Jesus loves and died for on the Cross. Thank God that He hasn't stopped healing the broken hearted and letting the oppressed go free.

> *Ps. 34:17-18   The Lord hears his people when they call to him for help. He rescues them from all their troubles. 18 The Lord is close to the brokenhearted; he rescues those whose spirits are crushed. NLT*
>
> *Matt 10:8   Heal the sick, raise the dead, cleanse those who have leprosy, drive out demons. Freely you have received, freely give. NIV*

Forgiveness

Paul & Lynn Crawford

Forgiveness changes more than earthly comprehension can grasp. Unforgiveness is a sin that harms and oppresses the perpetrator and the victim. Forgiveness and unforgiveness affect our perspective on everything. With unforgiveness, we see the worst in the situation and in the people involved. Through forgiveness, we see consideration, empathy, understanding, compassion, belief and God's love.

> *1 John 1:9* *"But if we confess our sins to him, he is faithful and just to forgive us and to cleanse us from every wrong." (NLT)*

God's Forgiveness is complete.

When we ask for His forgiveness, it's also forgotten. That lie, immoral act, theft or mean deed is removed from the record forever in God's sight. His blood completely washes it away. If you are ever reminded of your forgiven sin, it's not God reminding you.

> *Heb. 8:12* *"And I will forgive their wrongdoings, and I will never again remember their sins." (NLT)*

Resist Re-hashing What Has Been Forgiven

Satan will use your memory to remind you of your sin, in order to negate what God has done for you. Allowing the evil one's reminders in your thoughts will make you less effective in attaining an overcoming life led by the Holy Spirit. Stop it in your mind so it doesn't enter into your spirit. You are free. The Word says it. Believe it.

> *2 Cor. 2:10-11*   *"When you forgive this man, I forgive him, too. And when I forgive him (for whatever is to be forgiven), I do so with Christ's authority for your benefit, so that Satan will not outsmart us. For we are very familiar with his evil schemes." (NLT)*

Forgiving Brings Release

Our forgiving releases both our self and the forgiven party. The longer the time there is between the offense and granting forgiveness, the more pain you will endure. We don't have the ability to forget as God does. It takes time for the pain to subside, but it starts the minute you forgive.

Time Heals

It is a pleasure to get together with friends from the past. Last fall I met with a friend; as we reminisced I was asked about some very painful things from the past. I could not remember most of these events until they told me many of the details. When you don't feed it, the pain goes away and the painful memories grow dimmer. Eventually, you do forget with time and God's healing love.

> *Matt 6:14-15* *"If you forgive those who sin against you, your heavenly Father will forgive you. But if*

you refuse to forgive others, your Father will not forgive your sins." (NLT)

Mark 11:25 "But when you are praying, first forgive anyone you are holding a grudge against, so that your Father in heaven will forgive your sins, too." (NLT)

Luke 6:37-38 "If you forgive others, you will be forgiven. If you give, you will receive. Your gift will return to you in full measure, pressed down, shaken together to make room for more, and running over. Whatever measure you use in giving—large or small—it will be used to measure what is given back to you." (NLT)

Instant Forgiveness

Charles and Frances Hunter are bigger than life and are spiritual powerhouses. With no one else have I ever experienced such boldness in a husband and wife team that they demonstrate. Some people are offended by their aggressive evangelism and spiritual style. Often I have seen reactions towards the Hunters that were nasty and un-Christian. One of the greatest lessons Lynn and I learned from them was to choose to forgive *immediately. This* eliminates so much pain and stress. Your natural man wants to hold a grudge. You must train yourself and practice instant forgiveness. It is a supernatural thing.

Sometimes the Offender Doesn't Know

Sometimes you are wronged by ignorance, lack of knowledge or insensitivity. The offender may not even know they have offended you.

> Col. 3:13   "You must make allowance for each other's faults and forgive the person who offends you. Remember, the Lord forgave you, so you must forgive others." (NLT)

> Luke 23:34   Jesus said, "Father, forgive these people, because they don't know what they are doing." (NLT)

Offenses Never End, But Choose to Forgive. It Will Get Easier.

> Luke 17:3-4   "I am warning you! If another believer sins, rebuke him; then if he repents, forgive him. Even if he wrongs you seven times a day and each time turns again and asks forgiveness, forgive him." (NLT)

Restoration but not punishment

> 2 Cor. 2:6-8, 10-11: "He was punished enough when most of you were united in your judgment against him. Now it is time to forgive him and comfort him. Otherwise he may become so discouraged that he won't be able to recover. Now show him that you still love him... When you forgive this man, I forgive him, too. And when I forgive him (for whatever is to be forgiven), I do so with Christ's authority for your benefit, so that Satan will not outsmart us. For we are very familiar with his evil schemes." (NLT)

Unforgiveness Can Hinder Healing

Unforgiveness can hinder healing; the previous scriptures clearly tell us that we must forgive to receive the fullness of what God has for us.

Never Tell Someone They are not Healed Because of Unforgiveness

A sick and hurting person does not need your condemnation. If they are genuinely seeking God, allow the Holy Spirit to work. Often, the gift of the Word of Knowledge will bring something to the surface where it can be dealt with. When God has put someone in front of you seeking ministry, allow the Holy Spirit to operate through you in order to meet their need.

Inner Healing and the Healing of Memories

We deal with this in depth in our healing section; Inner Healing/Healing of Memories is generally due to a suppressed offense. One's current psyche may have buried its unforgiveness. I liken it to stuffing an offense and its pain down in a dark corner of your heart. In that dark place you don't deal with it and at some point you may forget it, at least temporally. You resist dealing with it because it is filled with pain.

Bring Offenses Into God's Light

Take the ministry time to allow the hidden offenses to come forth. Shine God's light, love, power and forgiveness upon it. Instruct them to ask God to show them anything that is hidden. This allows the offense to be addressed, forgiven and healed.

Testimony

In June of 2001, I was at a Spokane Healing Rooms Conference. At the end of the conference, a woman approached me; she said that she should have talked to me years ago about her experience. She and her husband have an International Ministry based in Idaho. She had attended our Seattle Forgiveness seminar 10 years ago and participated in the prayer. Like many other old-time Christians, she felt she had dealt with any need to forgive. As a committed Christian and minister, she has attended more than 50 conferences. Out of those 50 conferences, God had given her about 10 revelations that changed her life. The Forgiveness Prayer was one.

Please open yourself to the Healing that has come for many, from this prayer. It will touch areas of your life you never even considered that could or might need to be explored.

Forgiveness Prayer

> Lord Jesus Christ, today I choose to forgive everyone in my life. I know that You love me more than I love myself. Give me the desire and ability to forgive totally.
>
> Father, I forgive you for the times death, difficulties, or what I thought were punishments sent by You, came into the family. Sometimes people said *"It's God's will,"* and I became bitter and resentful...cleanse my heart and mind today.

Lord, I forgive MYSELF for my sins, faults and failings. I repent of any delving into horoscopes, going to séances, fortune telling, wearing lucky charms, I renounce any involvement with new age teaching, channelers, ESP, etc. I forgive myself... Your word says your people perish for the lack of knowledge...Give me discernment to recognize the traps of the enemy.

I also forgive myself for taking Your name in vain, not worshipping You in spirit and in truth, not going to church, hurting my parents, abusing alcohol or other substances, indulging in bad books or movies, fornication, adultery… homosexuality… leading children into impurity or abusing them emotionally or physically.

I forgive myself for committing abortion, murder, my part in the war, lying, stealing, defrauding, gossip, slander… I am truly sorry.

I forgive my MOTHER for the times she hurt me, resented me, and punished me too harshly. I forgive her for the times she preferred my brothers or sisters to me. I forgive her for the times she told me I was dumb, stupid, ugly, the worst of the children, that I cost a lot of money… For the times she told me I was unwanted, a mistake, an accident... not what she expected... I forgive her.

I forgive my FATHER for any non-support, lack of love,
 affection, nurturing or attention. I forgive him for
 not giving me his companionship, for drinking,
 fighting with my mother and all of us. I forgive him
 for the physical, emotional, sexual abuse... for
 severe punishments, for desertion, being away from
 home...divorcing my mother or running around...for
 all these things and any others...I forgive him.

Lord, I extend forgiveness to any SIBLINGS who
 competed for my parents' love or attention, hurt me
 physically, lied about me, rejected me... made life
 unpleasant for me...I forgive them.

I forgive my SPOUSE for lack of love, affection,
 consideration, support, attention, communication;
 for faults, failings, weaknesses and other acts or
 words that hurt or disturb me....

I forgive my previous SPOUSE or relationships for the pain
 they caused me and our children. I choose to
 forgive them for the abuses to me and the children:
 physical, emotional, sexual, anger and non-support.

I choose to forgive my CHILDREN for their lack of
 respect, obedience, love, attention, bad habits,

substance abuse, sexual permissiveness and sins, falling away from the Lord and the church, any other acts that disturb me... I forgive. Relatives; aunts, uncles, in-laws, grandchildren… Neighbors... Co-workers… Employers.

I forgive Government/Political Parties and Politicians, Religious denominations that harassed, attacked argued, tried to convert me, forced their views on me....and asked me for money.

I forgive Professional People, who may have hurt me in any way; doctors, nurses, lawyers, judges, civil servants....I forgive all service people, policemen, bus drivers, medical workers, and repairmen who have taken advantage of me.

I forgive School teachers or Instructors who called me dumb, humiliated me, treated me unjustly, and made me stay after school.

Lord, I forgive FRIENDS who have let me down, lost contact with me, were not there when I needed them, borrowed money and didn't repay it, or gossiped about me

I especially pray for the grace to forgive that ONE PERSON in my life who has hurt me the most. I forgive anyone I consider my greatest enemy, the one who is hardest to forgive, or the one I vowed I would never forgive.

Thank You, Jesus. I am free of the evil of unforgiveness. Holy Spirit, fill me with your light and love in every dark area of my heart and mind. AMEN.

Divine Pardon

By Lynn Crawford

One day while in a meeting with a group of women, I inquired of the Lord, "*What do you want to do now, Lord?*" As I waited, I listened for a Word of Knowledge, which is one of the gifts of the Holy Spirit God promises. (1 Cor. 12)

> *1 Cor. 12:7-11   A spiritual gift is given to each of us so we can help each other. 8 To one person the Spirit gives the ability to give wise advice; to another the same Spirit gives a message of special knowledge. 9 The same Spirit gives great faith to another, and to someone else the one Spirit gives the gift of healing. 10 He gives one person the power to perform miracles, and another the ability to prophesy. He gives someone else the ability to discern whether a message is from the Spirit of God or from another spirit. Still another person is given the ability to speak in unknown languages, while another is given the ability to interpret what is being said. 11 It is the one and only Spirit who*

distributes all these gifts. He alone decides which gift each person should have NLT

"*Injured in an accident,*" this thought popped into my head. I'm learning to just trust that it is from God, and speak it out. Most of the time, someone does respond and God heals them. The risk of looking silly if no one does come forward is there, but it is far better to trust, and speak it out. "*Is there someone here in pain as the result of an accident?*" In a way, I was expecting something connected to a car accident, but I'd actually only "heard" the word accident, not any specific type. A young woman in the back raised her hand. I asked her to come forward, assuring her God wanted to touch her. I gave her a big hug. It takes a bit of courage to come forward in front of everyone.

While hugging her, I whispered, "*It's all right, God has something really special for you tonight.*" Then I asked her name and what had happened to her. "*Annie*", she told me, *I crashed through a sliding glass door when I was just a child. I have permanent nerve damage and there's been these shooting pains in this arm ever since.*" She pushed her sweater sleeve up revealing a nasty jagged scar that ran along the inside her arm. While she was speaking, I got an inner sense from the Holy Spirit. I like to call it a divine download from God. Someone connected with this incident had hurt her emotionally and now was the time to deal with her wounded heart. The Holy Spirit is God. He is all love, all mercy and all knowing. I'm just a regular believer, learning how to recognize His leading. I'm still in His divine school.

So I innocently asked, "*Is there someone connected to this injury that you need to forgive?*" The dam that was holding back all her pent up anger and sorrow broke. "*I can't,*" she cried in tears. "*I just can't. I've already let go of a lot of stuff. This is* asking too much. He was wrong," she cried, even more outraged. "It was his entirely his fault. He was supposed to be watching out for me, but he caused it by goofing off and acting stupid. He's still doing it. He hasn't learned a thing and somebody is always getting hurt. Forgive him? I can't. I just can't." She crumbled in my arms, still crying the tears of that innocent child hurt by someone she trusted to keep her safe. *"Lord, I silently prayed, Give me Your words for Annie. What do you want me to do, Lord?"* Then with Daddy God gently leading me, I carefully repeated the words I heard Him deposit in my heart. *"Lord, right now, let Annie experience Your love, way down deep in her heart, thank you, Lord, for loving us first. Thank you for the Cross, Lord."* I felt God wrap us in His love like a blanket. She grew quiet and was calm. It reminded me of the scripture, *"He will quiet you with His love (Zeph. 3:17). "Do you feel that, Annie?" "Yes"* she whispered. Heads were nodding everywhere. We were all under His Divine Comforter together. *"That's God,"* I said, *"answering our prayer. Let's all thank Him for His presence right now."* Gentle declarations of love and gratitude filled the room and rose all the way to the Throne Room as we basked in His presence. Safe in His divine embrace, I continued. *"Yes, Lord, we thank you for the Cross. Look at the Cross, Annie. Look at all Jesus did for you. He died for you. He paid the full penalty for every sin you ever committed. Anything that could ever separate you from God, Jesus took it all away with His Blood. Do you see that, Annie?"* Again she nodded yes. *"He paid for every sin you committed and every sin committed against you. That's why He chose the Cross. For you, Annie, He did it for you. Do you see that?" "Yes,"* she replied. *"Even this-Jesus bore the full punishment for this sin committed against you when you were just a little girl. He shed His Own Blood to atone for this. Is His Blood enough?" "Yes,"* she said, *"Oh Yes" "So because of the Cross, because of the Blood He shed, Jesus asks us to forgive. We all have to let go of our need to punish those who have hurt us. We need to let go of the grudge and be willing to forgive. It wasn't good. It wasn't right. It wasn't fair. But if you choose to obey His command to forgive, Jesus will help you. Can you choose to forgive now?"* She solemnly declared, *"Yes."* *"Good, Annie, that's good."* Just repeat this prayer after me.

"God, today I chose to forgive -------." She repeated putting his name in. *He wasn't careful. He really didn't know what he was doing, he didn't know the damage he caused to my body, my soul, my heart; I forgive him and trust you God to deal with him. I choose to release all hurt and bitterness attached to this incident. I let it all go because of Jesus, because of the Cross. When he comes to my mind, I will pray for God's love to fill him and heal him. I will choose blessing and not the curse of rehashing this accident over and over again. I trust you, God, to restore our relationship when he's truly trustworthy. Until then, I will love and bless him from a safe distance. I thank you, Lord, today I am completely free of unforgiveness."*

As she repeated this prayer, the sense of God's peace grew stronger and stronger. In that atmosphere of God's love and mercy, we knew we were truly on Holy ground. In awe, we all said *"Amen. So be it"*

We'd just seen God create a clean heart and renew a spirit right before our eyes! (Ps.51:10) Annie broke into a huge smile. *"It's gone. The pain is completely gone. I can't believe it. I've been in constant pain for over 20 years and now it's gone. It's really gone."* We all rejoiced that God's healing power didn't stop with her arm but went all the way to her heart. It's amazing. It's God. It's true. When I read Matt. 9:5-8, I can see there is a powerful connection between the forgiveness of sins and healing.

Col. 3:13 says, readily pardoning each other as the Lord has freely forgiven you

Eph. 4:31-32 says, Let all bitterness be banished from among you, be kind to one another, tenderhearted, and freely forgiving one another as God in Christ forgave you.

Anybody can hold on to a grudge. But it takes a king, a president, a judge or an obedient child of God to grant a pardon. As members of God's family, His very own royal priesthood, He has given us the authority to heal and forgive. Time after time in scripture, and in our life, we have seen proof that the authority to forgive and heal is closely knit together. It's never too early or too late to forgive. It's a choice to obey God's Word and let go of those old hurts that hold us back from experiencing all God has for us.

Matt.18:22 reminds us that forgiveness is a "seventy times seven commitment," and forgiveness calls us back to the Cross again and again. Never give up. There is no limiting what God can do for you when you decide to get off the judgment seat and live in mercy. Our faithful God promises that the benefits of mercy extend to a thousand generations to those who love Him and keep His commandments. (Deut. 7:9) When we share that same mercy, there is a unique blessing as well as a special satisfaction and joy. This mercy is what we all received when Jesus paid the full price for our sins and failures and made us His own. I think that's why Jesus said, *"Blessed are the merciful, for they shall obtain mercy. Blessed are the pure in heart for they shall see God." (Matt 5:7-8)*

Loving Yourself God's Way

Lynn Crawford

It's a good thing I don't love my neighbor as I love myself. I'd be arrested for assault! But I don't think I'd be alone. Most of us would never dare say aloud the things we internally say to ourselves when we make a mistake. Even if my neighbor had a Great Dane that pooped in my yard, I still wouldn't stomp over and call him an idiot. But that is what I call myself when I'm standing in the parking lot and I don't have a clue where I parked my car. Or better yet, when I get home and realize I forgot to pick up the one item that I went to the store to buy in the first place. Forgiving myself for being human, that's a biggie.

One day over lunch, a friend shared how she had struggled with an accusing inner voice. *"I deal with the same thing,"* I said. Whenever I have an opportunity to share God's love, whether I am speaking to a group or just one person, it's there telling me, '*You don't deserve to share Jesus. You're not good enough,*' "I try to push through and just carry on in spite of it, but it's always there weighing me down," I confided. *"I know how to get rid of it,"* she said. *"I did, and you can to."* She continued, *"A friend asked me to fill in for her as the main speaker at a women's retreat. Even before I agreed to go, that voice started in,"* '*You can't do this. You're not prepared. They want her, not you. This isn't going to be good.*' "On and on it went until finally I prayed. I love you

Jesus. I want to share Your love, the love You've shown me, with these women. I believe this is an open door from You. So thank you for sending me and using me to share Your gospel, So off I went." She explained how God gave her the "peace that passes all understanding" ruling in her heart. *"The very first night I spoke straight from my heart. Trusting the Holy Spirit, I shared some of the dark times when God had met me. My struggles with illnesses, my husband losing his job, even the troubles we went through with our children. I've been tested and boy do I have a testimony! I'm still standing; God's love never fails! The healing and restoration we experienced in our own families is evidence."*

Her message of hope rang true for enough hurting women that first night to fill the altar, and God met each one, bringing comfort and strength. It was good. It was God.

"I went to bed that night." she said, *"thanking God as I remembered all He had done. In my heart; I heard that beautiful still small voice whisper, "Well done, beloved. Well done." "Smiling, I fell asleep in His arms."*

She explained how the retreat committee asked to see her the very next morning, and how she talked within herself, *"Why do I always feel like I'm going to the principals office and I'm in big trouble?"* She said the memory of God's embrace pushed her insecurity to the side lines. The committee spoke to her, *"We are not happy about last night. That is not the way we do things here. We are very disappointed; your talk did not follow an outline and there was way too much emotionalism. We just don't think you're right for our group. We know you meant well, and we do appreciate you coming, but we'll take it from here."* She said she left as gracefully as she could, and that on the inside, she agreed with them. She continued, *"As soon as I closed the door, in the safety of my room, I lost it. I'm so sorry God, I could barely get* the words out I was crying so hard, I failed You. I didn't study enough or pray enough. I'm not as good a speaker as she is. Why did I think I could do this? I was wrong to come. She's prettier, she's smarter, she sings better than me. She's even thinner than me."

She told me that instead of the sweet comfort she expected, she heard the heavenly Father's gentle rebuke. *"Be quiet my daughter. I am weary of your self-loathing. I am pleased with how I made you. You are fearfully and wonderfully made. (Ps.139:14) I chose to make you just as you are. Your personality, your voice, even your laugh and the color of your eyes, everything exactly according to My divine preference. I want you, my daughter, to show forth my praise in a unique way. I want you to sing a new song that only you can sing. For I long to hear your voice, I want to see your face. Your voice is sweet to me and your face is fair (Song of Songs 2:14). I love you. I accept you. I forgive you just the way you are. Repent of rejecting my handiwork. Stop hating yourself. You don't' have to be perfect. Accept yourself right where you are, failures and all. I do. I love you. Be kind, tender-hearted, forgiving yourself as I, Christ Jesus, have forgiven you."* (Eph. 4:32). She did and the accuser was evicted!!

    I know this to be true because this is my story too. The same put downs and accusations hammered me and maybe you too. If that's the case, pray this prayer out loud…

    "Jesus, I repent of hating myself and how you made me. That means I'm going to stop being hard on myself. Teach me how to accept myself and lean on You in my weakness. Convict me when I start beating myself up again. Because of the Cross, I choose to forgive myself. Thank You Lord. I am free of all unforgiveness, even not forgiving myself. Show me how to confess, repent, forgive and rejoice in the abundant life You've given me.

Thank you Jesus, because of you, I'm totally loved, totally accepted and totally forgiven. Amen. So be it. The accuser is gone."

Renewing my mind to this better way of thinking is a daily process. Being released from judgment is MIRACULOUS!! Be patient with yourself. God's not finished with you yet!

Faith Stretchers

Lynn Crawford

    The Monsignor poked my husband in the chest, punctuating every word, *"I want you to heal him."* Paul's brow was damp, and it wasn't from all the high humidity and tropical heat. Carlos sat in the front row smiling patiently. He was always the first to lend a helping hand setting up extra chairs or even locating a fan so we Americans wouldn't melt in the intense Philippine heat. He had polio, as a child, leaving him with an atrophied right leg three inches shorter than the other. He used crutches in order to get around. But that didn't stop him from being one of the most effective and dearly loved leaders in the Charismatic renewal circle in Cebu. If anyone's own goodness earned their healing, Carlos definitely deserved to be healed. But he would be the first to remind us it is only through Jesus we are saved and divinely healed.

    The Monsignor said *"Many famous healing evangelists from America,"* then he named some very prominent preachers you would know, some that intimidated Paul, *"they have prayed for him and still he is not healed. I want you to heal him."* His authoritative tone was not to be ignored. *"HELP LORD, HELP!!"*

How did we get into this situation? Easy, it all started when we became good friends with a Catholic priest who loved the Lord and shared our desire to build relationships upon the things that we as Protestants and Catholics have in common, instead of our differences. Together we all preached and ministered healing and forgiveness to the leaders in the Charismatic movement. We called our team ONE IN THE SPIRIT. That is the process that led to us minister in the Philippines. We were training leaders so they could in turn, minister healing as well as be the healing teams in a large healing service which was to be held in Cebu that Sunday. We had seen many healings in our training sessions and expected to see much more. But a specific miracle for a specific person? I'll admit, I was a little worried, though I tried not to show it.

"All right, Monsignor," Paul assured him, *"we'll be sure to minister to Carlos today."* Silently, we were both praying that same desperate prayer, *"HELP LORD, HELP!!!* We carried on with the afternoon's scheduled sessions. After a time of sweet praise and worship, we had a time of sharing; God had already been healing in our training sessions, so it was exciting to hear how several people had been instantly healed and were now pain free. God was encouraging all of us and building our faith. Paul taught a session on *Knowing Who You Are in Jesus.* (1 John 4:4) says it best-*The greater One is in you and me!* It's not about us. It's all about Jesus in us!! Next, I taught, *Conquering Your Fear of Moving Out;* we were really preaching to ourselves. Several times, there were these divine nudges, and we would act on them. *"I sense God wants to heal a neck problem."* The person would come forward and we'd minister to them and God would heal them. The pain would go instantly, and mobility would return. We all praised God as He continued to demonstrate His love and power again and again. Meanwhile, Carlos sat front row center,

celebrating each healing with a huge grin on his face, hopefully waiting for his time.

Late that afternoon we presented our *Forgiveness Teaching and Prayer*. This is one of the most powerful segments of our teaching, as many people let go of debilitating old hurts. Next, we presented our section on *Infirmity and Spiritual Warfare*. We had given almost all we had in order to impart to these believers that they may minister, and still Carlos sat there quietly smiling. All that remained was to Anoint and Commission them according to Mark 16:17-18, that they would go out preaching the gospel and laying hands on the sick. The next day, these same believers would be the ones ministering at the Healing Explosion held in their large sports arena.

Paul looked directly at Carlos. *"We'd like to take this time to minister to Carlos. You all know him and love him and we can see why. Carlos, you are definitely a man after God's own heart. Would it be alright if we prayed for you?"* *"Yes, of course, I'd like that."* With difficulty, He awkwardly made his way to the far side of the stage and up the three stairs. Every eye was glued to the center of the stage as Paul set up a folding chair and invited Carlos to sit down. Some people that were in the back stood on chairs to get a better look. No one wanted to miss a thing. Paul looked intently at Carlos and prayed, *"Lord, You know Carlos, how he is truly a beloved brother, never letting his physical difficulties limit his service for you. I thank You Lord that You paid the full price for his healing. In the Name of Jesus Christ, and by the power of the Holy Spirit, I bind you spirit of infirmity and I command you, Polio, leave this man now in the Name of Jesus. I command this leg to be strengthened and all these muscles to be fully restored over night in Jesus Name. Thank You God, You hear me and You already paid the full price for Carlos and his total healing. Amen!*

Amen! So be it!" Spontaneous shouts of praise and applause for all God had done filled the room. Carlos stood up and hugged Paul, smiling and thanking God. He then made his way off the stage looking exactly the same, encouraged by that special sense of God's love for him, but still on crutches.

We concluded our commissioning of the healing teams and went back to our room for dinner, and to rest up for the next day. We talked about the many visible healings we'd seen and how so many were relieved of severe pain. *"Maybe I didn't have the faith so see Carlos's leg instantly healed,"* Paul confided. *"It came into my heart to ask for an overnight miracle. So that's what I did. Now, I just need to leave it all in God's hands."* We still don't know why some aren't healed, but we've learned to focus on the healings that are received and trust God with the rest. He's the Divine Physician. We're just following His orders.

The next day was wonderful chaos. There were lots of people streaming into the auditorium for healing as well as last minute sound problems to fix. It always comes together somehow. We had pre arranged for a number of people to share how God had healed them. Everyone was so excited. Then someone asked us, *"Have you seen Carlos today?"* *"No not yet,"* we answered. Then they pointed to the opposite side of the stage. Here came Carlos without crutches, smiling and running to Paul. They hugged and Carlos jumped up and down on his new leg! Only a little limp! There was absolutely no weakness. Overnight, God had made him whole. Praise God!!! Carlos was one of the first to testify that morning. With joy he said, *"Lynn, yesterday you sang that song about Jesus asking us to dance. I've never been able to dance for the Lord before today. Could we do that now?? Dance for Jesus?"* I could barely see through my tears of joy as we twirled and bounced and danced like never before. Everyone in that auditorium danced, sharing Carlos' first dance with Jesus. Unforgettable!!!

That was the first of many miracles we were privileged to see that day. Blind eyes opened to see for the first time, people getting up out of their wheelchairs and walking, tumors dissolved and again, Carlos having his very first dance on a healed leg.

A song I wrote says: -- *"Our God delights to play new songs with bruised reeds, and He loves to dance with crooked feet made straight, and He likes to take the foolish things and confound the wise. With our God it's never too late."*…Not even for an overnight miracle!!

The Catholic Connection

Paul Crawford

My first contact with a Catholic priest was Fr. Benedict Grochel. He was teaching at a Seminary in Yonkers, NY. This was around the time that I began searching for God's will for my life. I had an interview in Miami with a national women sportswear manufacturer. When I left Miami I knew the job was not for me. I changed my plane ticket and flew to Newark, NJ, and got a hotel for the night. I had no idea what I would do next, but was searching and praying. I turned on the television and there were six priests sitting in a circle talking about the upcoming Catholic Charismatic event in Yankee Stadium. The language, phrases and spiritual focus sounded like my Pentecostal background. The only name I caught was Fr. Benedict Grochel. I called the number on the screen and was able to get Fr. Grochel's office number. It was 8am and I told him I must see him. He told me to come to Yonkers and have lunch at 2pm. Getting from New Jersey to Yonkers was a challenge for a West Coaster. I met him following his last class. He told me we would be having lunch at a Cloistered Convent on the campus. I had no idea what that was. He explained that these Cloistered Nuns never came out in public but devoted themselves to prayer and were undefiled by society. He took me into a small room with a table that could seat four at the most. There was a small counter and a slit in the wall where food was set out for us. I told him my background and how the previous evening television program had impacted me. I told him I had never met a priest, and my background avoided Catholics like a plague. I wanted to be honest with him and my ignorance and prejudices poured out.

I told him that South American missionaries stayed in my home and said Catholics killed protestant missionaries and threw rocks at their church during meetings. The picture I had of Catholics was from a trip to Mexico City, where I saw people crawling on their knees to the Shrine of Guadalupe; that gave me the impression they were heathens. I told him I knew these views were wrong based on what I had heard on the program. I wanted to understand Catholics and their beliefs. He suggested I visit Fr.Tichner, the Catholic Charismatic liaison in Southern California. I got a flight that night to Los Angles.

As an early riser, I was ready at 7am and drove the few miles from the airport to the Southern California Catholic Charismatic headquarters. I arrived before 8am and no one was there. Around 9am, the office worker said Fr. Tichner would arrive soon. When I met Fr. Tichner, I told him I had been sent by Fr. Grochel and I wanted to learn about Catholics. He said he would be busy until after the 10am Mass. He invited me to join the Mass. I informed him I did not know when to stand and when to sit. He assured me I didn't have to worry about that and he would guide me. There were about eight of us that took part of my first Mass. It didn't turn out to be foreign to me at all. It started with a greeting and then the Penitential Rite:

Priest: As we prepare to celebrate the mystery of Christ's love, let us acknowledge our failures and ask the Lord for pardon and strength.

All: I confess to almighty God, and to you, my brothers and sisters, that I have sinned through my own fault, in my thoughts and in my words, in what I have done, and in what I have failed to do; and I ask blessed Mary, ever virgin, all the angels and saints, and you, my brothers and sisters, to pray for me to the Lord, our God.

Priest: May almighty God have mercy on us, forgive us our sins, and bring us to everlasting life.

All: Amen.

I couldn't relate to the Mary part but the rest sounded like a "Born Again" prayer. The most important is asking God for forgiveness, admitting your sins and you are a sinner, stating you believe in and are pledging to follow Christ. There were prayers, then a reading from the Old Testament followed by a Psalm. In between these were responses from the participants. Then we all stood for the reading of the Gospel. Fr. Tischner held up the Bible high as a point of focus. Following the Gospel reading he lifted up the Bible and then kissed it as it was placed on the table. I had never seen such respect shown the Word of God. Next was the Homily, which was Fr. Tichner's teaching on the Gospel reading of the day. After the Homily, there were more responses from the people including quoting the Apostles Creed. The apostles Creed was total foreign to me. I had never heard it, knew what it was or knew what it meant.

      In 310 A.D., the church leaders called a meeting. In that time, the Church had many different splinter theologies, and they wanted to have one position they all could agree on. The resulting

Apostles Creed (below) was the adopted doctrine of the Church, and is part of the mass:

I believe in God, the Father Almighty, the Creator of heaven and earth, and in Jesus Christ, His only Son, our Lord: Who was conceived of the Holy Spirit, born of the Virgin Mary, suffered under Pontius Pilate, was crucified, died, and was buried. He descended into hell. The third day He arose again from the dead. He ascended into heaven and sits at the right hand of God the Father Almighty, whence He shall come to judge the living and the dead. I believe in the Holy Spirit, the Holy Catholic Church, the communion of saints, the forgiveness of sins, the resurrection of the body, and life everlasting. Amen.

This was followed by the Eucharist or communion as I knew it. Catholics believe that when the bread and the wine are prayed over (consecrated), they spiritually become the body and blood of Christ. This theological point is called *"Transubstantiation."* The Catholic communion is closed to non-Catholics. When you come forward for communion you are not asked if you are a Catholic. I believe this opens the door for many non-Catholic's to take communion in the Catholic Church. I personally think it would be an offense to the Catholics to participate if you do not believe in *"Transubstantiation"* or reject it as a possibility. This is followed by taking the bread and the wine.

This was just the beginning of our relationship with Catholics. Lynn and I have had many ministry opportunities in Roman Catholic settings with Catholic priests, Bishops and Cardinals. On two separate "God incidents" I actually shook hands with Pope John Paul.

China

Paul Crawford

I have had the privilege to provide help to many ministries in China. It all started in the Philippines where Lynn and I were conducting *"Gods Healing Power Through You"* seminars. The first Christian leadership delegation to make a foreign visit was lead by Bishop Ding. Bishop Ding was an Episcopal Bishop before 1950 when most churches were shut down with church leadership, pastors, Bible ladies, priests, nuns and many others imprisoned.

In the early 1980's, China started to open up and allow Chinese leaders to visit other countries. Most were released from prison or under house arrest and some churches were allowed to reopen; as directed by the Communist party Religious Bureau. Under the bureaus' control was the Three Self Church representing all Protestants. The second organization was the Catholic Patriotic Church.

Methodist Bishop Castro, of Manila, had become a good friend to us. He had invited the Chinese delegation to the Philippines, and had the responsibility to host them for a week. His budget was limited and he wanted to put on a banquet for their last night at the Sheraton hotel. He asked me if I would pay for the banquet. We had been blessed by publishing over ten books of other authors in the Philippines which provided for the banquet. I had no idea how expensive a Peking Duck banquet for thirty people would cost. But we saw once again, God always provides. I sat next to Bishop Ding during the dinner. At that time, I was producing television programs in Manila. When Bishop Ding learned about my video production he invited me to the China Christian Council headquarters and National Seminary in Nanjing.

The China Christian Council had an agreement with the World Bible Society to setup the first China approved Bible printing since the 1950's. The invitation was to videotape the startup of the printing presses about six months later. The Bible Society provided the presses, the installation and the paper. The China Christian Council operated the business that provided three hundred local jobs. The Bible Society operations manager was from New Zealand. When the day to startup arrived, I was in Nanjing. This was the first of more than thirty trips I have taken to China. During my stay, I videotaped the startup and many of the publishing operations. These included typesetting, making the covers, the complete print process, binding and the final assembly with finished Bibles rolling out on a conveyer belt. This was a great day for me and the Kingdom of God.

When I returned to the states my recordings were shown on two Christian networks. Immediately I began to receive critical letters that I had been duped and this was only propaganda. Some were even from some well known ministries who have done an outstanding job supplying Bibles in China. I wrote an article for Charisma magazine. Charisma and I received many letters saying this was not true, that it was Communist propaganda damaging the work of ministries that smuggled Bibles into China. One key Hong

Kong ministry told me to stay out of China, because they had worked in China for twenty years.

To date, over 40 million Bibles have been printed on the Nanjing presses. Many of the ministries that told me I was duped are now having there Bibles printed in China. I have personally taken thousands of Bibles that I declared to Chinese customs. Chinese customs required the destination of the Bibles. I took over 1000; one side English, one side Chinese Bibles to Shanghais University. Many Jesuit priests taught there, and used the Bibles to teach English.

Bishop Ding had a fondness for Skippy Peanut Butter which was not available in China until the mid 1990's. Every China trip I would lug two large jars of Skippy for Bishop Ding. If I was not scheduled to visit Nanjing, I would ship it to him from Beijing, Shangri or Hong Kong. I didn't need to tell him, it was coming and he knew who it was from.

On my early trips into China I was followed wherever I went, or the taxi had to report where he had taken me. When I arrived at a seminary they would have to report that I had been there. Chinese would have to register with the government get a Bible. By 1990, the China Christian Council opened Bible book stores in some major cities; there are now there are over 70. As with before, the Bible stores required you to register. In the late 1980's, you could get Bibles, study Bibles and Bibles on tape without registration. In the early 1990's, the churches were allowed to put Bible tables on the street in front of their church where anyone could buy them. As you can see, over time, great changes have come to China.

I met a woman in Hong Kong named Susan Woodman. She had worked in China, when it was first opened up in order to visit church leadership to provide them some resources and encouragement. Susan told me that I had to meet the Catholic Bishop of Shanghai, Aoulsis Jin. Bishop Jin had been released two years earlier from twenty six years of imprisonment. When the Communists took over he was in Rome attending seminary. During that time, he also trained in France. Bishop Gong in Shanghai told him not to return as he most likely would be arrested. He chose to return and was put in charge of the Shanghais Seminary. Within a few months, Bishop Gong and Fr. Jin were arrested and imprisoned. Ten of his twenty six years were in solitary confinement without a Bible. Little do we Westerners know or understand about faith developed in solitary confinement. When I met Bishop Jin, I knew he was a man of God. His heart was to serve God and his fellow Chinese.

    I had a sponsorship from the Catholic Charismatic Foundation in Eindhoven, Netherlands. This allowed me to invite Bishop Jin to visit the United States. The sponsorship covered the travel for the Bishop as well as a seminarian to accompany him. They flew into Los Angeles, CA, where I picked them up. I had arranged for Bishop Jin to stay at a parish, of Dominick, the Southern California Catholic Charismatic area leader. That afternoon I put him in Dominick's charge. A few days later, we moved on to Seattle. I took him to visit Bishop Hunthousen where they commiserated about the problems they both had in serving the people, and with their leadership. They had a grand time, as if they were lifelong friends.

    The next destination was to visit the Seattle University Jesuit Vicar General at the Jesuit residence hall. The Vicar General came down from his room, but would not shake hands or acknowledged Jin as a Bishop. I couldn't figure out what was going on. Bishop Jin knew so he took the Vicar around the corner and did not return for an hour. When they returned they were best of friends.

The next stop was to visit the Dominican Fathers at Blessed Sacrament Church and attend their Gregorian Mass. After I delivered him to the Dominican Fathers, I called the Jesuit Vicar and asked him what the fuss was about. He informed me that his Vicar General in Rome had advised the Jesuits in the United States of Bishop Jin's impending visit. They were not to recognize him as a Bishop or say Mass with him as he was not part of the underground Catholic Church. I knew he would be saying Mass with the Dominican Fathers so I called Fr. Ryan, Bishop Hunthousen's chancellor. I asked him if it was okay for Bishop Jin to say Mass with the Dominican Fathers. He said he would call me back, and he did so with a "no," but it was too late.

Then we were off to Dayton University in Ohio. We flew to Ohio and were accommodated at one of the local rectories. Bishop Jin was to speak at the University that evening, I did not go but took the evening to catch up and rest. As I sat in the living room with the parish priest, He asked me why he had received a letter from Cardinal Ratzinger informing all Dioceses that I was to bring Bishop Jin around the United States, and that they should shun him. This all seemed so strange to me as an Assembly of God preacher's kid. My faith was challenged; had I heard God and followed his leading by hosting this trip? Now Rome seemed unhappy with me. I prayed about it but got no relief. That night, I called my sponsor in Holland and told them my fears. During this time, Cardinal Ratzinger was the Defender of the Faith for the Catholic Church. My sponsorship could call him as they knew him well, sponsoring many of his projects. The next morning I received a call advising me that this was political and I was doing a good job. Today Cardinal Ratzinger is the Pope.

Sister Rosie's Creative Miracle

Lynn Crawford

The years haven't diminished the glowing memory I have of Sister Rosie and her miracle. Paul and I were in our second day of teaching our *"God's Healing Power Through You"* seminar when I met her. I was returning to the stage area after our lunch break when a woman from the prayer group intercepted me and asked if I could come with her to pray for a nun who was very ill. Of course I agreed to go, and followed her down a covered walkway to the library. A border of huge exotic plants and flowers ran along both sides. I could hear what I thought was a bird calling, *"kah-kowe kah-kowe,"* it sounded really close. So I asked, *"What kind of bird is that?"*, *"That's no bird, it's a lizard."* Yikes!! I didn't want a lizard to jump out at me or run across my foot so I really got a move on. Sister Rosa Lee was sitting in a big chair waiting for us in the library. She was so tiny, I'm 5'3" and when they helped her to her feet, she barely came to my shoulder. Her friend spoke English so she told me Sister Rosa was over 80 years old and had served over 30 years in China. She was having severe heart problems so the doctors sent her back to the Philippines to closely monitor her condition. Sister Rosa was homesick for China and the ones she'd left behind, however she resigned that this was God's will.

I could see that she was God's special treasure. All those years she trusted God, far away from the familiar, her home and family.

> *1 Peter 1:7   These trials are only to test your faith, to show that it is strong and pure. It is being tested as fire tests gold—and your faith is far more precious than mere gold. So if your faith remains strong, after being tried by fiery trials, it will bring you much praise and glory and honor on the day when Jesus Christ is revealed to the whole world.*

I could see the resulting faith in her, and it was humbling. I asked if I could pray for her and she said, *"Yes, of course."* She was very weak, but stood up with help. I took each of her gnarled hands in mine, asked her to look at me and keep her eyes open. *"Thank you, Lord, for Sister Rosa and her love for You that over flowed into her service with You in China. Thank You for the many who came to personally know You, Jesus, through her."* I placed my hand over her heart. *"I bind you, Satan, and all your attacks on her health and heart in the Name of Jesus."* I was going to command repair to her all of her heart, when a unique boldness came over me from the Holy Spirit causing me to say, *"I command a new heart to come into Sister Rosa right now, in the Name of Jesus, a teen-age heart. A teen-age heart with new strength, new passion, and a brand new heart that's even more in love with You, Jesus."* Sister Rosa was over whelmed with God's power and started to swoon. The people, who had been supporting her, gently lowered her to the floor. Some concerned friends rushed to her side. But she waved them off with a huge grin. *"I'm ok"* she said in English. The color had returned to her cheeks and she did look really good. *"Are you sure you're all right, Sister Rosa,"* I asked. Through tears of joy she told me, *"Yes, I'm fine. But please, don't call me Sister Rosa anymore. From now on I'm Sister Rosie! I feel like a teen-ager!! I have a new heart."* She got to her feet and began to do a little dance of joy. We all joined her, laughing and clapping and celebrating God's healing power. Sister Rosie danced and danced with new strength and vigor. Minutes before, she'd been unable to walk or even stand on her own. Wiping away my tears of joy, I had to pull myself away and get to the next healing session. God had just performed a creative miracle and given a precious nun a new heart, but that was only the beginning of the amazing miracles we would witness in Cebu that week.

FGBMFI Japan

Paul Crawford

    Seattle Full Gospel Business Men's Fellowship International director, Bob Bignold, asked me to scout out Japan to establish FGBMFI Chapters. Years before there had been some chapters but they had been disbanded. I was conducting four tours a year to Israel. We planned that I would go from the end of an Israel trip to visit missionary friends in India and then on to Tokyo. When I arrived in Tokyo, I met with an elderly man that was part of the previous Tokyo chapter. He told me of the problems with an American style organization operating in the Japanese social structure. There were many challenges. The main challenge being that Japanese men worked late, getting home from 9-10pm, plus working most of Saturday. If they were Christians they only had Sunday for their families and rest.

    Through this elderly man I found Kaz Suzuki. Kaz was interested and knew about FGBMFI from a trip to the United States. From there I went to Osaka and met Noel Morris a missionary from New Zealand. Noel's primary work was recording Christian conference and church events. Through his work he knew many Christian leaders in Japan. Through Kaz and Noel, I setup the future first meetings in Tokyo, Osaka and Kobe. Some were general introduction meetings, some were ministry oriented and others were the typical banquet meetings.

The FGBMFI ministry setting was to have a banquet where a member would invite an unbeliever from a business relationship, or a personal friend. At FGBMFI banquet meetings, it was normal to bring wives, but in Japan women were not part of a man's world outside the home.

When I met with a major Tokyo hotel about holding a banquet they acted strange when I told them it would be with couples. I presented the plans to Kaz and he also acted strange. I asked him what the problem was. He stated that spouses did not go out to evening functions. I questioned why. The answer was that Japanese families do not have babysitters unless a grandparent lives in the home. Many missionaries in Japan told me that you couldn't do "this or that" within the Japanese culture. As I pushed on, I saw that in God's plan cultures and traditions can be overcome by the Holy Spirit.

On my return home, Bob Bignold from the Seattle FGBMFI, planned a trip to Japan for the two of us. On arrival in Tokyo, we met Kaz who had setup a meeting the following day with a group of men. When we arrived at the meeting no one came. We spent a few hours in prayer and moved on to Osaka. Bob and I were both confirmed Episcopalians so Noel Morris used this relationship to set up an introductory meeting at an Episcopal Church. On arrival about ten people were there and it swelled to thirty. Most all were senior citizens, many were women. I introduced the FGBMFI and our plans for Japan. Bob took over and started teaching on faith, and things that he had seen God perform. These were salvation for the "worst of the worst," deliverance, healing and miracles. He then told about legs growing out and backs being healed.

This was early in my faith walk and I had not ministered healing up to that point. I didn't approve of the leg thing as a ministry style. I knew from the direction Bob was going he was going to do the leg thing. I went to the back of the room and prayed *"God don't let Bob do this, the Japanese won't go for it. I will be embarrassed and you God will be embarrassed. Bob won't be embarrassed because he doesn't understand the Japanese culture."* As I prayed I heard Bob say *"Is there anyone here with a bad back in pain now."* A bent over elderly lady with two walking canes stood up. Bob ask her to come forward and she hobbled up. Bob put her in a chair and measured her legs. One was about 1½ inches shorter, and she had extreme pain. Then to add to my embarrassment, he asked if anyone had seen a miracle. Every person in the place came forward and huddled around Bob to see the legs. He showed them the difference in length and told them to watch them grow when he ministered. His words were something like this: *"I command the back to straighten, and I curse the pain in Jesus name."* As he did this the legs became the same lengths as the back straitened. The people watching made audible noises of exclamation. He told her to stand up and bend over. She stood up straight and bent over and said there was no pain. Without her canes she jumped up and started running from the front to the back of the church many times.

      I returned to the back of the church and asked God to forgive me for putting him in a box, limiting what I thought He could do. The next night there were two meetings scheduled. Bob asked me to take one of them. It was in a church and most Japanese churches were small at that time. But this church was big and had fifty seats where most churches had attendance of about twenty. I had never been the only one leading a meeting before. This would require me to speak and minister. The pastor asked me to meet him at 5pm. When I arrived we viewed the church sanctuary and he took me out for dinner next door.

On returning from dinner the church was packed. I was excited and apprehensive because I thought they had come to hear me. The pastor had me sit on the little platform during the worship. As I looked around I saw the elderly lady that was healed the previous night sitting in the back row. I became fearful when I realized the room was full because of her testimony. I knew they all expected me to heal the needs that were present.

As I spoke I avoided looking at her. My words to the assembled were one thing but my real inner cry was *"GOD HELP."* I kept repeating the inner cry *"HELP, HELP, HELP"* and more *"HELP."* Then the moment came. I asked for anyone in severe pain that needed healing to come forward. A sixteen year old boy came forward. He had arthritis in his knees. It was all he could do to walk slowly the pain was so intense. I copied Bob and commanded the knee joints be restored, cursed the pain and arthritis and commanded it to go in Jesus name. I could see at once as his face immediately indicated the pain was gone. He testified the pain was gone and his knees were free. He also ran from the front to the back many times. Everyone that came forward that night was healed. My introduction to a personal healing ministry had happened. Lynn and I have conducted our seminar a dozen times in Japan with a great response in healing and spiritual growth from the people.

Months later we returned to Japan with a team from Canada. Canada had taken a leading role in FGBMFI Japan for some years. Later, I brought Charles and Francis Hunter to Japan which was instrumental in boosting FGBMFI Japan, and grew their annual conventions to an attendance of up to 5000.

Creating a Healing Atmosphere: Praise!

Lynn Crawford

Wherever Jesus is, there is healing. Where two or more are gathered in His Name, He's there. He's present in His Word. And He also inhabits the praises of His people. *Ps. 22:3 "But You are holy, Enthroned in the praises of Israel". W*hen I need healing, I especially seek out prayer meetings and anointed worship services. Wherever Jesus is, I want to be.

As I mentioned in the chapter, *"Franco Set Free"* I suffered an ectopic pregnancy, was hospitalized, and needed emergency surgery. I know it doesn't make sense, spiritually, but it happened. The peace of God held me so close during the ambulance ride to the hospital, and during all the preparations for surgery. I asked God, *"Am I going to heaven?"* I didn't get an answer, just this sense to just trust Him. I woke up cocooned in His loving presence.

Paul brought some of my Vineyard worship tapes and I played them over and over again. When I woke up I'd hear God's whisper *"Come to My healing place."* I knew that meant to put a worship tape on. Sometimes I worshipped along in my heart. Most of the time, I just lay there, soaking in God's love and healing in that environment of praise. I was in a Catholic hospital so I got a lot of prayer from the nurses and priests. That was a huge blessing. But whenever I was alone, I'd hear that divine invitation, *"Come to my healing place."* And I would come and stay there for hours. The doctor told us that I would be ten days in the hospital, and another two weeks before I would be able to fly back home. I wanted to get home to my children so badly, but I just kept going back to the "healing place" God had for me. God accelerated my recovery and I was released that Friday, only four days after surgery! I saw the doctor for a follow up that following Monday. He knew I wanted to get home as quickly as possible so he thought I was hiding the pain I was in. He privately took Paul aside. *"After this type of abdominal surgery, Lynn should still be walking all stooped over from the pain. I know she's just walking up right in front of me so I'll release her to fly home." "No, that's the way she's been walking,"* Paul assured him. The doctor said it was impossible, but with God, nothing is impossible. I had no pain, just a little soreness, similar to pain you would get when you've done too many sit ups. Praise God! Two days later, I flew home to my children! It was a miracle!

God has a healing place for you too. Give thanks to him and praise his name.

> *Ps. 100:4* Enter his gates with thanksgiving; go into his courts with praise.

Enter His gates with thanksgiving: Thank Him (out loud) for Who He is, being with you, loving you, keeping you. You don't have to be thankful for the problem, but be grateful He is there with you IN the midst of your storm.

Enter His courts with praise: Brag about what God has done for you. Boast about His faithfulness, rave about His love. Sing up beat songs to Him, lift up your hands, clap and dance before Him. You can do all this privately in your own home. It's just as powerful and you'll be creating a healing place with Him.

Give thanks to Him and praise His Name*:* Look for what has improved, don't focus on symptoms that may remain. Just say, *"Thank you Lord, the pain is less, my joints aren't as inflamed, I'm more flexible. I can walk longer than yesterday."* Some healings are immediate, some are progressive. But it's still God and He's healing you in His own way.

From the very beginning of my Christian walk, little songs and tunes would come into my head. Sometimes a scripture I was reading would begin to replay in my head as a song. So I'd sit down with my guitar and just let the words and chords flow. Or as I went about my daily tasks I would sing to the Lord my prayer concerns and praises. When an area of my life didn't seem to be growing I would sing over it. In Isaiah 5 He says, *"I will sing for the one I love, a song about His vineyard"* or Isaiah 54:1 *"Sing O barren, enlarge your heart and your home, make room for MORE of what God has for you"* (I'm paraphrasing). More love, more healing, more effective ministry, more fruit for the Lord! In Numbers 21:17, Israel sang this song: *"Spring up, O well!"* So I thought, I can sing over anything, my family, my church, my city, releasing God's well of salvation, His Rivers of life, springing up and overflowing in healing and renewal.

When I served as Outreach VP on the North Sound Aglow Area Board, I sang over our region for a new Aglow to be birthed, new wells of salvation for the women there. I was so immersed in this type of song intercession, I even got pregnant!! My son Joel, was born that year along with several new Aglows!

Almost fifteen years ago, we were doing video production for a conference in Edmonton, Alberta. This was an event with

Christians showing support to Israel. I met some amazing Holocaust survivors; one of them, a General, was actually born on the ship "the St. Lewis." I was overwhelmed by their stories of courage and sacrifice.

Alone in my room, I felt impressed to pray for Israel, but was feeling very inadequate. I turned to Jeremiah 30 to read for myself some of the verses the speakers had brought out. As I read, I thought, *"I know I should pray for Israel. It's vital. But, I don't even know how to begin. Help me Lord."* Then I heard God whisper in my heart, *"Sing my promises over Israel. Sing over my vineyard."* Starting in Jeremiah, 31:1, I began to sing, *"In that day, says the Lord, I will be the God of all the families of Israel. Yes, in that day," declares the Lord, "I will be the God of all the families of Israel. And they will be my people. Yes, they will be my people, they will be my very own people"* declares the Lord. Verse 2 became another song, then verse 7, and on and on the songs came finally resolving in verse 10. *"He who scattered Israel will gather them, gather them, He will gather them. He who scattered Israel will gather them and watch over His flock like a shepherd. Hear the word of the Lord, O nations. Hear the word of the Lord. He who scattered Israel will gather them and watch over His flock like a shepherd."* To my surprise, I'd been singing these song prayers for over two hours. It seemed like only minutes had passed. I said *"Thank you, Lord, for the songs You gave and this powerful way I can pray, I'm so grateful."* He said *"If you value what I give you, I'll give you more."* This promise has been so important to me as I learn to walk in the Spirit. Be grateful for what God has given you, and He'll give you more! More prayer opportunities, more gentle nudges, more words of knowledge, more prophetic songs. MORE!

I keep paper with me to capture what He gives, but a tiny digital recorder makes it easy to record the melody so nothing is lost. I'm in the process of learning piano. I needed more than six strings to echo the songs I heard in my spirit. I sit at the keyboard, tune my heart to Him and the songs just come.

Praying for my church during our building program, a song came that I privately sang for months. Then I shared it with my friend, Leilani. She's not only our pastor's wife, but also our worship leader, and a much anointed musician. She gave it some much needed polish that made it easier to sing. *"Come Make Our Praises Your Throne"* was warmly received at the dedication service for our new building. What a blessing!

God will do the same for you. Just begin. Right where you are, give Him ten minutes. Let Him lead you to a verse, or pick one that speaks to you. Then allow the Holy Spirit to direct your voice. It's like singing in the Spirit, but you're singing scriptures or the words He gives you. Remember, God's words always agree with His written word. You'll be amazed as His Rivers of Living Water overflow, causing the desert areas to bloom in your own life.

Categories of Healing

Paul Crawford

John Wimber impacted the church during the 1970's and 80's with his seminars and book, Power Healing. Lynn attended some of his first conferences and I produced his conference media in England and Scandinavia. His motto was *"do the stuff,"* which meant get out of the pew, witness and lay hands on the sick. Charles and Frances Hunter always said, *"If Charles & Frances can do it (heal the sick), you can too."* You don't have to be special; anyone can act on God's Word.

John Wimber described the Categories of healing as:

Healing of the Spirit

Definition: Healing of the spirit is renewal and restoration of your spiritual life, your relationship with God. Sickness of the spirit is caused by an individual's own sin. The first and deepest kind of healing is forgiveness which God provides in response to sincere repentance. Receiving salvation results in the healing of our spirit. An on-going experience of His forgiveness keeps us spiritually healthy.

King David's spiritual sickness and healing

King David, instead of going to war, was at home being tempted by sexual desires.

> 2 Sam. 11:2   "Late one afternoon, after his midday rest, David got out of bed and was walking on the roof of the palace. As he looked out over the city, he noticed a woman of unusual beauty taking a bath." NLT

His sin was adultery with Bathsheba

> 2 Sam. 11:3-4 "He sent someone to find out who she was, and he was told, "She is Bathsheba, the daughter of Eliam and the wife of Uriah the Hittite. 4 Then David sent messengers to get her; and when she came to the palace, he slept with her."

This resulted in pregnancy which led David to cover up his sin. He brought her husband home to make it appear as if the baby was his.

> 2 Sam. 11:6-13   "Then David sent word to Joab: "Send me Uriah the Hittite." So Joab sent him to David. 7 When Uriah arrived, David asked him how Joab and the army were getting along and how the war was progressing. 8 Then he told Uriah, "Go on home and relax." David even sent a gift to Uriah after he had left the palace. 9 But Uriah didn't go home. He slept that night at the palace entrance with the king's palace guard. 10 When David heard that Uriah had not gone home, he summoned him and asked, "What's the matter? Why didn't you go home last night after being away for so long?" 11 Uriah replied, "The Ark and the armies of Israel and Judah are living in tents, and Joab and my master's men are camping in the open fields. How could I go home to wine and dine and sleep with my

wife? I swear that I would never do such a thing." 12 "Well, stay here today," David told him, "and tomorrow you may return to the army." So Uriah stayed in Jerusalem that day and the next. 13 Then David invited him to dinner and got him drunk. But even then he couldn't get Uriah to go home to his wife. Again he slept at the palace entrance with the king's palace guard." NLT

By this time his sin effected relationships and lead to murder

2 Sam. 11:14-17   So the next morning David wrote a letter to Joab and gave it to Uriah to deliver. 15 The letter instructed Joab, "Station Uriah on the front lines where the battle is fiercest. Then pull back so that he will be killed." 16 So Joab assigned Uriah to a spot close to the city wall where he knew the enemy's strongest men were fighting. 17 And when the enemy soldiers came out of the city to fight, Uriah the Hittite was killed along with several other Israelite soldiers.

The sickness of the spirit caused physical discomfort

Ps. 38:4-6   When I refused to confess my sin, my body wasted away, and I groaned all day long. 4 Day and night your hand of discipline was heavy on me. My strength evaporated like water in the summer heat. NLT

David also suffered emotional and mental turmoil

Ps. 51:8,12   Oh, give me back my joy again; you have broken me—now let me. Restore to me the joy of your salvation, and make me willing to obey you. NLT

God's answer was to confront the sin through Nathan

> *2 Sam. 12:1-8 the Lord sent Nathan the prophet to tell David this story: "There were two men in a certain town. One was rich, and one was poor. 2 The rich man owned a great many sheep and cattle. 3 The poor man owned nothing but one little lamb he had bought. He raised that little lamb, and it grew up with his children. It ate from the man's own plate and drank from his cup. He cuddled it in his arms like a baby daughter. 4 One day a guest arrived at the home of the rich man. But instead of killing an animal from his own flock or herd, he took the poor man's lamb and killed it and prepared it for his guest." 5 David was furious. "As surely as the Lord lives," he vowed, "any man who would do such a thing deserves to die! 6 He must repay four lambs to the poor man for the one he stole and for having no pity." 7 Then Nathan said to David, "You are that man! The Lord, the God of Israel, says: I anointed you king of Israel and saved you from the power of Saul. NLT*

Confession and repentance was David's reply

> *Ps. 32:5   Finally, I confessed all my sins to you and stopped trying to hide my guilt. I said to myself, "I will confess my rebellion to the Lord." And you forgave me! All my guilt is gone.*

> *Ps. 51:1-4   Have mercy on me, O God, because of your unfailing love. Because of your great compassion, blot out the stain of my sins. 2 Wash me clean from my guilt. Purify me from my sin. 3*

For I recognize my rebellion; it haunts me day and night. 4 Against you, and you alone, have I sinned; I have done what is evil in your sight. You will be proved right in what you say, and your judgment against me is just. NLT

This confession brought God's forgiveness

Ps. 32:5   Finally, I confessed all my sins to you and stopped trying to hide my guilt. I said to myself, "I will confess my rebellion to the Lord." And you forgave me! All my guilt is gone. NLT

And healing of the spirit

Ps. 51:10   Create in me a clean heart, O God. Renew a loyal spirit within me. 11 Do not banish me from your presence, and don't take your Holy Spirit from me. 12 Restore to me the joy of your salvation, and make me willing to obey you.

And body

Ps. 51:8   Oh, give me back my joy again; you have broken me—now let me rejoice.

Healing of past hurts

Definition: While sickness of the spirit it caused by what we do, sickness of the emotions is generally done by others to us. It grows out of hurts done to us by another person or some experience we have been exposed to in the past. These hurts affect us in the present, in the form of bad memories, and fragile or wounded emotions. This in turn leads to various problems, depression, a sense of worthlessness and inferiority, unreasonable fears and anxieties, psychosomatic illness, etc. Included in this, are the present day effects of the sins of the parents, in the bloodline of the person.

Healing past hurts touches the emotions, the memories and the person's bloodline.

Peter's denial of Jesus

Because Peter set his heart on mans interest, he could not understand why Jesus had to die.

> Matt. 16:22-23   22 Peter took him aside and began to rebuke him. "Never, Lord!" he said. "This shall never happen to you!" 23 Jesus turned and said to Peter, "Get behind me, Satan! You are a stumbling block to me; you do not have in mind the things of God, but the things of men." NIV

He fought to the end in Gethsemane, but when Jesus was led away, Peter followed from "afar off" showing his despair and disillusionment.

> Luke 22:54-55 54 So they arrested him and led him to the high priest's home. And Peter followed at a distance. NLT

Peter's faith faltered, and three times he denied knowing Jesus. This caused immediate condemnation and his emotional reaction, bitterly weeping in deep depression.

> Luke 22:62   And Peter left the courtyard, weeping bitterly. NLT

It is clear that because of the trauma of Jesus' crucifixion, Satan was trying again to gain access to the disciples through their emotional crisis, but Jesus prayed for Peter.

> Luke 22:31-32 "Simon, Simon, Satan has asked to sift each of you like wheat. 32 But I have pleaded in prayer for you, Simon, that your faith should not

fail. So when you have repented and turned to me again, strengthen your brothers." NLT

After his resurrection, Jesus personally came to heal Peter's past hurt

He met Peter where shame and despair had driven him, fishing. First, through the miracle of the large haul of fish, Jesus brought back to Peter the positive memory of his calling, renewing his hope.

> *John 21:1-8 Later, Jesus appeared again to the disciples beside the Sea of Galilee. This is how it happened. 2 Several of the disciples were there— Simon Peter, Thomas (nicknamed the Twin), Nathanael from Cana in Galilee, the sons of Zebedee, and two other disciples. 3 Simon Peter said, "I'm going fishing." "We'll come, too," they all said. So they went out in the boat, but they caught nothing all night. 4 At dawn Jesus was standing on the beach, but the disciples couldn't see who he was. 5 He called out, "Fellows, have you caught any fish?" "No," they replied. 6 Then he said, "Throw out your net on the right-hand side of the boat, and you'll get some!" So they did, and they couldn't haul in the net because there were so many fish in it. 7 Then the disciple Jesus loved said to Peter, "It's the Lord!" When Simon Peter heard that it was the Lord, he put on his tunic (for he had stripped for work), jumped into the water, and headed to shore. NLT*

Secondly, Jesus asked Peter three times, "Do you love me?"

> *John 21:9   When they got there, they found breakfast waiting for them—fish cooking over a*

charcoal fire, and some bread. 15 After breakfast Jesus asked Simon Peter, "Simon son of John, do you love me more than these?" "Yes, Lord," Peter replied, "you know I love you." "Then feed my lambs," Jesus told him. 16 Jesus repeated the question: "Simon son of John, do you love me?" "Yes, Lord," Peter said, "you know I love you." "Then take care of my sheep," Jesus said. 17 A third time he asked him, "Simon son of John, do you love me?" NLT

John 18:17-27 The woman asked Peter, "You're not one of that man's disciples, are you?" "No," he said, "I am not." 18 Because it was cold, the household servants and the guards had made a charcoal fire. They stood around it, warming themselves, and Peter stood with them, warming himself. 19 Inside, the high priest began asking Jesus about his followers and what he had been teaching them. 20 Jesus replied, "Everyone knows what I teach. I have preached regularly in the synagogues and the Temple, where the people gather. I have not spoken in secret. 21 Why are you asking me this question? Ask those who heard me. They know what I said." 22 Then one of the Temple guards standing nearby slapped Jesus across the face. "Is that the way to answer the high priest?" he demanded. 23 Jesus replied, "If I said anything wrong, you must prove it. But if I'm speaking the truth, why are you beating me?" 24 Then Annas bound Jesus and sent him to Caiaphas, the high priest. 25 Meanwhile, as Simon Peter was standing by the fire, they asked him again, "You're not one of his disciples, are you?"

> *He denied it, saying, "No, I am not." 26 But one of the household slaves of the high priest, a relative of the man whose ear Peter had cut off, asked, "Didn't I see you out there in the olive grove with Jesus?" 27 Again Peter denied it. And immediately a rooster crowed. NLT*

Jesus simply believed Peter's hesitance, yet honest commitment *"Lord, you know that I love you,"* and he re-commissioned him to feed His sheep. This healed Peter emotionally, which in return renewed him spiritually and relationally.

Healing of the Body

Definition: Sickness of the body has its root in physical factors, either organic or functional disorders. Therefore healing of the body means changing and restoring the physical condition, so the body functions properly. Of all the kinds of healing, physical healing is the most difficult for us to believe in. It seems far easier to pray for something spiritual than something physical.

> *Mark 2:8-10 Is it easier to say to the paralyzed man 'Your sins are forgiven,' or 'Stand up, pick up your mat, and walk'? NLT*

Miracles frequently happen in areas of healing of the body

> *John 9:6-7 Then he spit on the ground, made mud with the saliva, and spread the mud over the blind man's eyes. 7 He told him, "Go wash yourself in the pool of Siloam" (Siloam means "sent"). So the man went and washed and came back seeing! NLT*

Blind Bartimaeus: Mark 10:46-52

Blind Bartimaeus' healing took place in public alongside the road.

> *Mark 10:46-52   Then they reached Jericho, and as Jesus and his disciples left town, a large crowd followed him. A blind beggar named Bartimaeus (son of Timaeus) was sitting beside the road. 47 When Bartimaeus heard that Jesus of Nazareth was nearby, he began to shout, "Jesus, Son of David, have mercy on me!" 48 "Be quiet!" many of the people yelled at him. But he only shouted louder, "Son of David, have mercy on me!" 49 When Jesus heard him, he stopped and said, "Tell him to come here." So they called the blind man. "Cheer up," they said. "Come on, he's calling you!" 50 Bartimaeus threw aside his coat, jumped up, and came to Jesus. 51 "What do you want me to do for you?" Jesus asked. "My rabbi," the blind man said, "I want to see!" 52 And Jesus said to him, "Go, for your faith has healed you." Instantly the man could see, and he followed Jesus down the road.*

His blindness had affected his social relationships, he was a beggar. Mark 10:46

Faith had made him whole. Mark 10:52

His faith was characterized by:

1. Determination, boldness and persistence.
2. He saw Jesus for Who He really was, *"The Son of David"*
3. He believed in God's mercy.

Jesus asked what he wanted. Mark 10:51

Jesus healed him through the spoken word and he was healed immediately. Mark 10:52

Healing of the Demonized

Definition: Sickness caused by demonic influence can have some of the symptoms of the first three categories (spiritual, emotional and physical). Therefore the healing of this type of sickness requires the expulsion of the demonic influence and the restoration of all effective areas.

The Syro-Phoenician woman's daughter

This woman came to Jesus on behalf of her daughter who was demonized. There is no mention of the nature of the demonization.

> Mark 7:25-26 Right away a woman who had heard about him came and fell at his feet. Her little girl was possessed by an evil spirit, 26 and she begged him to cast out the demon from her daughter. NLT

Her faith was the main factor in her daughters healing. The mother had amazing persistence and shamelessness. She also trusted in the mercy of God.

> Matt 15:23-28 But Jesus gave her no reply, not even a word. Then his disciples urged him to send her away. "Tell her to go away," they said. "She is bothering us with all her begging." 24 Then Jesus said to the woman, "I was sent only to help God's lost sheep—the people of Israel." 25 But she came and worshiped him, pleading again, "Lord, help me!" 26 Jesus responded, "It isn't right to take food from the children and throw it to the dogs." 27 She replied, "That's true, Lord, but even dogs are

> *allowed to eat the scraps that fall beneath their master's table." 28 "Dear woman," Jesus said to her, "your faith is great. Your request is granted." And her daughter was instantly healed.NLT*

Jesus pronounced the healing

> *Mark 7:29-30 "Good answer!" he said. "Now go home, for the demon has left your daughter." 30 And when she arrived home, she found her little girl lying quietly in bed, and the demon was gone. NLT*

The amazing thing is the healing took place over some distance. The demon left the child when Jesus spoke some miles away.

Healing of relationships and healing of the dying

Definition, Healing of relationships: God has given us precepts to order our relationships one to another. The violation of the precepts results in broken relationship. Therefore the healing of relationships comes with an exchange of forgiveness and reapplication of the precepts. Harmonious relationships contribute to the health of the whole community.

Definition, Healing the dying: Death is ultimately man's enemy, so the first steps towards healing of the dying is the proper understanding of death. The idea is to bring people through the experience of death, both for the dying and the bereaved.

We have no model, it's all conjecture

Centurion's servant

Matt. 8:5-13   When Jesus returned to Capernaum, a Roman officer came and pleaded with him, 6 "Lord, my young servant lies in bed, paralyzed and in terrible pain." 7 Jesus said, "I will come and heal him." 8 But the officer said, "Lord, I am not worthy to have you come into my home. Just say the word from where you are, and my servant will be healed. 9 I know this because I am under the authority of my superior officers, and I have authority over my soldiers. I only need to say, 'Go,' and they go, or 'Come,' and they come. And if I say to my slaves, 'Do this,' they do it." 10 When Jesus heard this, he was amazed. Turning to those who were following him, he said, "I tell you the truth, I haven't seen faith like this in all Israel! 11 And I tell you this, that many Gentiles will come from all over the world—from east and west—and sit down with Abraham, Isaac, and Jacob at the feast in the Kingdom of Heaven. 12 But many Israelites—those for whom the Kingdom was prepared—will be thrown into outer darkness, where there will be weeping and gnashing of teeth." 13 Then Jesus said to the Roman officer, "Go back home. Because you believed, it has happened." And the young servant was healed that same hour. NLT

Nobleman's son

John 4:46-54   As he traveled through Galilee, he came to Cana, where he had turned the water into wine. There was a government official in nearby Capernaum whose son was very sick. 47 When he heard that Jesus had come from Judea to Galilee, he went and begged Jesus to come to Capernaum to heal his son, who was about to die. 48 Jesus asked, "Will you never believe in me unless you see miraculous signs and wonders?" 49 The official pleaded, "Lord, please come now before my little boy dies." 50 Then Jesus told him, "Go back home. Your son will live!" And the man believed what Jesus said and started home.   51 While the man was on his way, some of his servants met him with the news that his son was alive and well. 52 He asked them when the boy had begun to get better, and they replied, "Yesterday afternoon at one o'clock his fever suddenly disappeared!" 53 Then the father realized that that was the very time Jesus had told him, "Your son will live." And he and his entire household believed in Jesus. NLT

Woman with the hemorrhage

Mark 5:25-34 A woman in the crowd had suffered for twelve years with constant bleeding. 26 She had suffered a great deal from many doctors, and over the years she had spent everything she had to pay them, but she had gotten no better. In fact, she had gotten worse. 27 She had heard about Jesus, so she came up behind him through the crowd and touched his robe. 28 For she thought to herself, "If I can just touch his robe, I will be healed." 29 Immediately the bleeding stopped, and she could feel in her body that she had been healed of her terrible condition.30 Jesus realized at once that healing power had gone out from him, so he turned around in the crowd and asked, "Who touched my robe?" 31 His disciples said to him, "Look at this crowd *pressing around you. How can you ask, 'Who touched me?'" 32 But he kept on looking around to see who had done it. 33 Then the frightened woman, trembling at the realization of what had happened to her, came and fell at his feet and told him what she had done. 34 And he said to her, "Daughter, your faith has made you well. Go in peace. Your suffering is over." NLT*

Healing the dead

Definition: Resuscitation is the divine miracle of restoring a deceased person back to life. It is the rising of the dead back to a temporal life in the body, as opposed to the resurrection of the dead at the end of the age. It is a visible act of God's power which clearly shows his ability to invade Satan's stronghold and overpower him on his own turf.

Rising of Lazarus: Scripture listed below comment

Two Sisters sent a message to Jesus that Lazarus was ill, a plea for help. John 11:3

Jesus had a conviction (revelation) the ultimate issue of this sickness would not be death, but rather the revelation of the "Glory of God." Notice how calm and controlled His faith is from here on. John 11:4

Jesus knew God was in control, so although he loved Mary and Martha, he stayed there two extra days. He was not acting on external evidence but He waited on His Father. John 11:5,6

Lazarus died and then Jesus went up to Bethany. Jesus had a word of knowledge about his death. John 11:11-15

The purpose of raising Lazarus was to give Glory to God, inspire faith in the disciples and others, and to help Mary and Martha. John 11:4, 15, 35

The fact that Lazarus had been dead for four days means he was really dead. The spirit had left his body. John 11:39

Jesus first spent time comforting Mary and Martha by giving hope in faith in Him (God). He wept with them. John 11:21-40

Notice the terrible environment of unbelief, but Jesus was not affected because he had the Gift of Faith. John 11:33-40

Martha had faltering faith. John 11:22, 27, 29

Jesus did not pray for the resurrection but expressed gratitude to the father for the intimacy they enjoyed. John 11: 41, 42

He made preparation (prayer and rolling the stone away) and then he commanded in a loud voice "Lazarus come forth". John 11:43

The resuscitation resulted in spiritual renewal, emotional harmony, relationship restoration in the community and beyond. Do not forget it caused persecution as well. John 11: 45-48

> *John 11:1-48 A man named Lazarus was sick. He lived in Bethany with his sisters, Mary and Martha. 2 This is the Mary who later poured the expensive perfume on the Lord's feet and wiped them with her hair. Her brother, Lazarus, was sick. 3 So the two sisters sent a message to Jesus telling him, "Lord, your dear friend is very sick." 4 But when Jesus heard about it he said, "Lazarus's sickness will not end in death. No, it happened for the glory of God so that the Son of God will receive glory from this." 5 So although Jesus loved Martha, Mary, and Lazarus, 6 he stayed where he was for the next two*

days. 7 Finally, he said to his disciples, "Let's go back to Judea." 8 But his disciples objected. "Rabbi," they said, "only a few days ago the people in Judea were trying to stone you. Are you going there again?" 9 Jesus replied, "There are twelve hours of daylight every day. During the day people can walk safely. They can see because they have the light of this world. 10 But at night there is danger of stumbling because they have no light." 11 Then he said, "Our friend Lazarus has fallen asleep, but now I will go and wake him up." 12 The disciples said, "Lord, if he is sleeping, he will soon get better!" 13 They thought Jesus meant Lazarus was simply sleeping, but Jesus meant Lazarus had died. 14 So he told them plainly, "Lazarus is dead. 15 And for your sakes, I'm glad I wasn't there, for now you will really believe. Come, let's go see him." 16 Thomas, nicknamed the Twin, said to his fellow disciples, "Let's go, too—and die with Jesus." 17 When Jesus arrived at Bethany, he was told that Lazarus had already been in his grave for four days. 18 Bethany was only a few miles down the road from Jerusalem, 19 and many of the people had come to console Martha and Mary in their loss. 20 When Martha got word that Jesus was coming, she went to meet him. But Mary stayed in the house. 21 Martha said to Jesus, "Lord, if only you had been here, my brother would not have died. 22 But even now I know that God will give you whatever you ask." 23 Jesus told her, "Your brother will rise again." 24 "Yes," Martha said, "he will rise when everyone else rises, at the last day." 25 Jesus told her, "I am the resurrection and the life. Anyone who *believes in me will live, even after dying. 26 Everyone who lives in me and believes in me will never ever die. Do you believe this, Martha?" 27 "Yes, Lord," she told him. "I have always believed you are the Messiah, the Son of God, the one who has come into the world from God." 28 Then she returned to Mary. She called Mary aside from the mourners and told her, "The Teacher is here and wants to see you." 29 So Mary immediately went to him. 30 Jesus had stayed outside the village, at the place where Martha met him. 31 When the people who were at the house consoling Mary saw her leave so hastily, they assumed she was going to Lazarus's grave to weep. So they followed her there. 32 When Mary arrived and saw Jesus, she fell at his feet and said, "Lord, if only you had been here, my brother would not have died." 33 When Jesus saw her weeping and saw the other people wailing with her, a deep anger welled up within him, and he was deeply troubled. 34 "Where have you put him?" he asked them. They told him, "Lord, come and see." 35 Then Jesus wept. 36 The people who were standing nearby said, "See how much he loved him!" 37 But some said, "This man healed a blind man. Couldn't he have kept Lazarus from dying?" 38 Jesus was still angry as he arrived at the tomb, a cave with a stone rolled across its entrance. 39 "Roll the stone aside," Jesus told them. But Martha, the dead man's sister, protested, "Lord, he has been dead for four days. The smell will be terrible." 40 Jesus responded, "Didn't I tell you that you would see God's glory if you believe?" 41 So they rolled the stone aside. Then Jesus looked up to heaven and said, "Father, thank you for hearing me. 42 You always hear me, but I said it out loud for the sake of all these people standing here, so that they will believe you sent me." 43 Then Jesus shouted, "Lazarus, come out!" 44 And the dead man came out, his hands and feet bound in grave clothes, his face wrapped in a head cloth. Jesus told them, "Unwrap him and let him go!" 45 Many of the people who were with Mary believed in Jesus when they saw this happen. 46 But some went to the Pharisees and told them what Jesus had done. 47 Then the leading priests and Pharisees called the high council together. "What are we going to do?" they asked each other. "This man certainly performs many miraculous signs. 48 If we allow him to go on like this, soon everyone will believe in him. Then the Roman army will come and destroy both our Temple and our nation."*

Ten Actions Until Your Healing Manifests

Lynn Crawford

On certain occasions, I've been healed instantly, while some healings I received over time. In all these experiences, the result was still freedom. Free of the symptoms that were robbing me of that abundant life Jesus promises.

> John10:10 *"The thief's purpose is to steal and kill and destroy. My purpose is to give them a rich and satisfying life."NLT*

Here are some positive things you can do while you're in God's healing process.

1. ***Receive as much prayer as you can.*** Jesus told us, *"Don't get discouraged and give up but keep on! Keep on praying. Keep on seeking. Keep on believing."* (Paraphrasing Luke 18:1). When I was battling depression, we had a lot of warfare over a conference we were putting on. I got so discouraged; I just wanted to give up and crawl back under the covers. I was

pouring my heart out to God. I remember complaining, *"Lord, I must be crazy to let myself volunteer for all this pressure. I'm crazy. Or I'm just too dumb to quit."* Then the Holy Spirit said, *"Do you know what happens when someone is too dumb to quit? They win."* You are going to be completely healed either here on earth or in heaven. So don't quit!

2. **Keep praying the *"forgiveness prayer,"* at least twice a week.** I think forgiving is like restoring old furniture, sometimes you have to remove layers of gunk to get to the true grain of the wood. Some old hurts you may not even remember because you couldn't bear it. But as you grow in grace, experiencing more of God and His love, you'll be ready when the Holy Spirit reveals any hurts He wants to repair. Luke 4:17 records Jesus in the synagogue reading Isaiah 61:1-2.

> *"The Spirit of the Sovereign Lord is upon me, for the Lord has anointed me to bring good news to the poor. He has sent me to comfort the brokenhearted and to proclaim that captives will be released and prisoners will be freed. He has sent me to tell those who mourn that the time of the Lord's favor has come. "Jesus said," Today this scripture is fulfilled in your hearing."*

3. **Focus on the signs of improvement and thank God for each and every one.** Many healings are progressive, not instant. Never the less, they are still healings. The second you swallow an aspirin, your headache isn't gone. It takes some time. But aspirin companies are making a good profit because aspirin works.

> Rom. 4:19-20 *but he grew strong and was empowered by faith as he gave praise Abraham, not*

being weak in faith, did not consider his own body, already dead and in the deadness of Sarah's womb. Verse 20 (Amp Bible)

No unbelief or distrust made him waver or doubtingly question concerning the promise of God, but he grew strong and was empowered by faith as he gave praise and glory to God, fully satisfied and assured that God was able and mighty to keep His word and to do what he promised. Praise is the effective weapon to bring down the doubt and unbelief that fights against you. Watch out for those thoughts that start out with *"maybe"* or *"what if."* That's doubt talking. That's not belief. Praising God builds up your faith. *"Thank you, Father, today I have less pain. I can breathe better. I can walk farther. I have more energy and stamina. Thank you, Jesus. I'm better today than I was yesterday. I'm one day closer to my complete healing in Jesus Name!"*

4. **Meditate on God's Word.** Write out healing scriptures and highlight and plant specific scriptures in your heart. A Rhema Word especially sent from God to heal you. *Psalm 107:20 He sent His Word and healed them.* God's Word is ALIVE. God's Word has POWER. God's Word has purpose.

> *Proverbs 4:20-22   Pay attention my child, to what I say. Listen carefully. Don't lose sight of my Words. Let them penetrate deep within your heart for they bring LIFE and radiant HEALTH to anyone who discovers their meaning. God's Word is also your weapon in this battle. NLB*

> *Hebrews 4:12 For the Word of God is full of living power. It is sharper than the sharpest knife, cutting down deep into our innermost thoughts and desires.*

5. ***Guard your peace.*** The devil will lie to you. John 8:44 says he is a liar and the father of lies. Don't allow condemnation to rob you.

   > *John 10:10   The thief comes only to kill, steal and destroy; I came that you might have life, and have it more abundantly.*

   God has begun a good work in you and He will complete it! Philippians 1:6; 4:6, Romans 8:1.

6. ***Nurture an atmosphere of worship.*** Be grateful. Sing to the Lord, play worship music. God inhabits the praises of His people. Psalms 22. We go in to this more fully in our section *Create a Healing Atmosphere: Praise!*

7. ***Participate in communion.***

8. ***Stay in your doctor's care and follow his orders.*** Continue taking your medications. When you take your medications say *"Thank you God for these medications. Let them bless my body and accelerate my healing. I take them in the Name of Jesus. Amen."* If you are uneasy about a prescription, talk frankly with your doctor. If you are displeased or disappointed in the care you've received, forgive the doctor, then ask the Lord if this is the doctor you need or is there someone else. I needed to change doctors when I was prescribed an antibiotic I was allergic to. Instead of helping me through the reaction, he was more concerned I was going to sue him. So I forgave him and went to another doctor that gave me an antidote that put me back on the road to recovery. Your doctor is part of God's healing team. Your healing will stand up under medical examination. Remember, the Apostle Luke was a physician.

9. ***Present your body to God as a living sacrifice.*** Romans 12:1. This means all of you. Your mind, will, emotions and personality, give all of yourself to God. Let God transform you into a new person by changing the way you think. Rom 12:2. You may get an impression from God to drink more water, eat less sugar and more vegetables, and do more walking. Whatever He says, DO IT. Moderation is a fruit of the Spirit, and I've noticed the measures He recommends are usually not extreme, but balanced. Really ask Him to bless your food and drink. Don't fall into an empty ritual. There's much power in blessing.

10. ***Anticipate your healing.*** Maybe you've always wanted to go overseas on a mission trip, but your poor health prevented it. Go get your passport. Begin preparing for the day you will be able to go and preach the Good News, laying your hands on the sick and seeing them recover just like Mark 16:15-18. Declare, *"God has begun a good work in me and He will complete it."*

> *1 Thess. 5:23-24(The Message) May God himself, the God who makes everything holy and whole, make you holy and whole, put you together — spirit, soul, and body — and keep you fit for the coming of our Master, Jesus Christ. 24 The One who called you is completely dependable. If he said it, he'll do it!*

Declaring the Word Praying the Word

Paul Crawford

Now I lay me down to sleep. I pray the Lord my soul to keep. And if I die before I wake, I pray my soul, He'll take.

This was my first prayer. Over the years, from that first prayer, I have learned to pray in many ways. As an adult, I was very frustrated by prayer styles I could not maintain. In five minutes, I would have prayed for everything I knew was wrong and everybody who needed God's touch in their lives. I have two friends who described themselves as intercessors. They lived about 30 miles from me and they would ask me to pray with them when I was in their area. One was a pastor and the other heads a prayer ministry for men. They were real men of God and prayed for 6-8 hours a day. The pastor was building a new church and the interior finishing was delayed. They used this empty unfinished church for their prayer closet. It had no heat or air-conditioning so you dressed accordingly. At their insistence, I joined them a few times. Their prayer life style was 99% praying in tongues very loud. Very loud and very long. I lasted to the one hour break but really lasted only 10 munities. I tried again a few weeks later with the same results. I so respected them and I was ashamed I could not pray the way they prayed. I almost gave up any effort to develop an intercessory prayer life.

Some years later, I met Mike Bickle, the pastor of Kansas City Metro Church. For many years I produced the video at their conferences and Saturday night meetings. Mike was well known for prayer. Much of his prayer life developed as he cared for his quadriplegic brother. With hours to read the Word, meditate and pray he started praying and declaring the Word. Mike then established a prayer room, in the church upper level which was open whenever the church doors were opened. Then some people got keys so they could be in the prayer room when the church was closed.

Today, Mike heads the International House of Prayer, open 24/7 in Kansas City. I was there when it opened the first time. They have 2 hour sessions continually around the clock. The prayer model is declaring the Word, Praying the Word, Singing the Word and the prophetic. Each session had a Worship team, a prayer leader and an open microphone for the session attendees.

I was thrilled with this prayer model. I could participate in a 2 hour session and stay for more. Sometimes for many hours, the evening or the day, and then come back for more the next day. Over the past few years, I go to Kansas City IHOP for a few days. Typically, I combine it with a 100 hour fast. I then return to my daily life renewed both spiritually and physically.

Today Kansas City IHOP facility holds about 1000 people with evenings well attended and a few at 2am or 4am. You can experience K.C. IHOP on the Internet live or visit their facility.

This type of prayer has been established in prayer centers worldwide. The North America facilities are near 800 and over 100 internationally, including Jerusalem.

Today, I have four main prayer styles.

First: Declaring the Word   I can give you an example for this that occurred last Sunday. Our pastor called the congregation forward to pray for our community needs. There were concerns about wayward children of the congregation. I prayed: *"Father your Word says that if we raise them in the way, they will return. Father, we declare your Word to be true and we call them in!"*

Second: Praying the Word   I am listing some compiled by Mike Bickle with many more available from IHOP's website: http://www.ihop.org

APOSTOLIC PRAYERS OF PAUL

1. Prayer for revelation of Jesus' beauty and the Bride's destiny unto transforming our heart
...the Father of glory, may give to you the SPIRIT OF WISDOM AND REVELATION IN THE KNOWLEDGE OF HIM, the eyes of your understanding being enlightened; that you may know what is the HOPE OF HIS CALLING, what are the riches of the GLORY OF HIS INHERITANCE IN THESAINTS, and what is the exceeding GREATNESS OF HIS POWER TOWARD US who believe (Eph. 1:17-19).

2. Prayer for the release of supernatural strength in the heart unto experiencing God's emotions.
...that He would grant you, according to the riches of His glory, TO BE STRENGTHENED WITH MIGHT THROUGH HIS SPIRIT IN THE INNER MAN, that Christ may dwell in your hearts through faith; that you, being rooted and grounded in love, MAY BE ABLE TO COMPREHEND with all the saints what is the width

and length and depth and height-- to know the love of Christ which passes knowledge; that you may be filled with all the fullness of God. (Eph. 3:16-19)

3. Prayer for God's love to abound in our heart resulting in discernment and righteousness. *And this I pray, that YOUR LOVE MAY ABOUND still more and more in knowledge and all discernment, that you may APPROVE THE THINGS THAT ARE EXCELLENT, that you may be sincere and without offense till the day of Christ, being FILLED WITH THE FRUITS OF RIGHTEOUSNESS which are by Jesus Christ, to the glory and praise of God (Phil. 1:9-11).*

4. Prayer to know God's His will, to be fruitful in ministry and strengthened by intimacy with God. *We…do not cease to pray for you, and to ask that you may be filled with the KNOWLEDGE OF HIS WILL in all wisdom and spiritual understanding; that you may have a WALK WORTHY OF THELORD, fully pleasing Him, BEING FRUITFUL in every good work and increasing in the knowledge of God; STRENGTHENED WITH ALL MIGHT, according to His glorious power, for all patience and longsuffering with joy; giving thanks to the Father who has qualified us to be partakers of the inheritance of the saints in the light. (Col. 1:9-12)*

5. Prayer for unity within the church across a city or region. *Now may the God of patience and comfort GRANT YOU TO BE LIKE-MINDED toward one another, according to Christ Jesus, THAT YOU MAY WITH ONE MIND AND ONE MOUTH glorify the God and Father of our Lord Jesus. (Rom. 15:5-7)*

Third: Praying in Tongues Praying in tongues is your spirit communicating with God's Spirit without your understanding (mind) getting in the way. I use it anytime I am confronted with a prayer issue, that I don't know how to pray for. This can be my needs and concerns, for family, friends, my church, my nation and government.

Tongues have been a big release for me with issues I am frustrated with. An example would be abortion. Because I travel 180 days a year, I cannot be a regular participator on issue battles in my home region. To fill this need, I have travel prayer strategies. When my travels take me near Washington D.C., I take an extra day for a prayer walk. My prayer walks generally are alone around the Supreme Court, the Capital building and the senate office building. Often very few people are around so it just me communicating in the Spirit. I don't know what to pray but the Spirit will.

Fourth: Pray Without Ceasing The Word says we should pray without ceasing. I entered this realm about 15 years ago. Under my conscience, I am praying in the Spirit continually. Sometimes it becomes so intense I lose track of what I am doing. Lynn has learned to deal with this when I am driving. When she senses I am lost in the Spirit she will remind me we are on earth by helping me back to the conscious realm. We take the same route to our home whenever we go out. Before we get to the main turn she will say *"Are you going to turn?"* I often awake from sleep with my spirit praying to God's. I sometimes erupt into tongues out loud. I don't think you can find anybody that could say they saw me discouraged, rather the opposite, praying in the Spirit helps build you up.

Personalizing God's Word

Paul Crawford

From the cradle I was in Church. My first knowledge of bible things was Sunday school stories. These were presented by the teacher with many illustrations. I grew up thinking the bible was a history book about God and Jesus. Later I learned it was written by men inspired by the Holy Spirit but it still seemed like history.

I noticed my parents studying the bible all the time and I wondered how much they had to read to understand history. At age 13 I received the Holy Spirit into my spirit. Then the bible changed.

It took a lot of years and many mistakes to learn the Word was God's instruction manual for my life. We don't have to go through life without knowing what to do or our destiny. It's in the instruction manual.

 A big step I learned from Frances Hunter. Frances would mark out words like, we, us, they, his, elders, yourself, their, anyone, men, women, them, him disciples and write in Frances. I would write in

Paul and my wife Lynn. I have used my full name in bold to illustrate in an extreme way

An example is Mark 16:15-18 15 He said to **Paul Crawford**, "Go into all the world and preach the good news to all creation. 16 Whoever believes and is baptized will be saved, but whoever does not believe will be condemned. 17 And these signs will accompany **Paul Crawford** who believes: In my **name Paul Crawford** will drive out demons; Paul Crawford will speak in new tongues; 18 **Paul Crawford** will pick up snakes with **Paul Crawford** hands; and when **Paul Crawford** drink deadly poison, it will not hurt **Paul Crawford** at all; **Paul Crawford** will place their hands on sick people, and they will get well." NIV

Other examples: Acts 2:38-41 38 Peter replied, "Repent and be baptized, every one of you **Paul Crawford**, in the name of Jesus Christ for the forgiveness of **Paul Crawford** sins. And **Paul Crawford** will receive the gift of the Holy Spirit. 39 The promise is for **Paul Crawford** and **Paul Crawford** 's children and for all who are far off — for **Paul Crawford** whom the Lord our God will call." 40 With many other words he warned **Paul Crawford**; and he pleaded with **Paul Crawford**, "Save yourselves from this corrupt generation." 41 Those who **Paul Crawford** accepted his message **Paul Crawford** were baptized, and about three thousand were added to their number that day. NIV

Luke 24:49 9 I am going to send **Paul Crawford** what my Father has promised; but stay in the city until **Paul Crawford** have been clothed with power from on high."

Sometimes I need to use Lynn's bible and it says Lynn everywhere. I think or read it in when I study so mines not so marked up. The point is that you need to personalize each scripture for yourself. Add that concept and allow the Holy Spirit to be your teacher I can assure understanding and revelation will flow.

A few years ago a company started printing personalized New Testaments. You send him your name, parents and other family members. He will print you a complete personalized bible. Now they have 3 personalized pocket size, 80-100 pages, on healing, marriage and finances.

There website, **www.PersonalPromiseBible.com**, allows you to print out 2 samples (men or women) with your name inserted. An example of mine and Lynn's follows.

Try it and your faith will grow.

Declaring: Personalized Healing and Health Scriptures

We wanted to include healing scriptures that you can declare or pray. Personalized Promise Bible, who provided the Identity in Christ for a previous chapter, have a series of healing and health scriptures personalized. The following is the content of the pocket book personalized for myself.

The World English Bible was used for the following scriptures due to copyright and other concerns. If you have a verse speak to you, or one you don't understand review it in another translation. The main ones I use are King James. New Living Translation, Amplified, NIV and New King James. I also have a 26 translation parallel bible.

Faith comes by hearing. When you hear it or read it, with your name included it moves from you mind to your spirit. I believe this is the best thing to do as you wait for your healing to manifest.

Paul Crawford's **Personal Pocket Scriptures for Health & Healing Personal Promise Bible® Series. Based on the World English Bible**

Personal Promise Bible®

Published by: Phronesis International, 470 Heritage Hills Dr., Richland, WA 99352 **www.PersonalPromiseBible.com** Copyright © 2005 Phronesis International, Richland, WA

All rights reserved. *Paul Crawford* may copy or print the Personal Promise Bible® *By His Stripes* Personal Pocket Scriptures for *his* own use. Modification of the text specifically to customize for other names is prohibited.

ISBN 0-9759578-2-1 For additional Personal Promise Bible® products: Phone: (509) 627-2607 Toll Free:(866) 968-7242 (866-YOURBIBLE)

Introduction

We are so abundantly blessed by God's demonstration of His love in sending Jesus to absorb upon His body the penalty for our sins and to give us abundant life instead of death. Jesus told us in John 10:10b "*I came that **Paul** may have life and may have it abundantly.*"[1] The term abundant means super abundant in quantity and superior in quality. It is beyond measure. That's the power of the blood of Jesus for the healing of our physical bodies.

---

[1] To make these passages easier to read, we have italicized Jesus' words. Personalizations and text changes (other than minor grammatical changes) are shown in bold and italics.

We're told in Hebrews 13:8 that "Jesus is the same yesterday, today and forever." That's really good news because Acts 10:38 tells us "Jesus went about doing good and healing all who were oppressed by the devil." And then, Peter confirms in Acts 10:34 "Truly I perceive that God doesn't show favoritism."

If Jesus never changes and God doesn't show favoritism then, you can know for a surety that whatever was done in the Scriptures for somebody else, God will do it for you as well.

There are two Greek words used for salvation or saved. They are "soteria" which means health, preservation, rescue, safety, soundness, and deliverance from danger. The other Greek word is "sozo" which means healed, cured, preserved, made whole, made well, get better, and deliverance from suffering. Both of these words include eternal salvation as well as health and physical healing.

Because of the blood of Jesus we are now delivered from the power of darkness and all of the negative consequences of sin including sickness and death. Colossians 1:13-14 says, "He delivered **Paul** out of the power of darkness, and translated **him** into the kingdom of the Son of His love; in whom **Paul** has **his** redemption through His blood, the forgiveness of **his** sins." Being healed is being saved in the physical sense.

Health and healing are part of the covenant promises from the Old Testament through the New Testament. God healed in the Old Testament and gave us His Name as "Jehovah Rapha" (Exodus 15:26) and He told us in Malachi 3:6 "For I am the LORD, I do not change." We see that God continued to heal and bring wholeness through Jesus' ministry.

Hebrews 8:6 says, "But now He has obtained a more excellent ministry, since He is the Mediator of a better covenant, which has been enacted on better promises." How awesome to know that "God is not a man, that He should lie, nor a son of man, that He should repent. Has He said, and will He not do? Or has He spoken, and will He not make it good?" (Numbers 23:19-20a.)

Health and healing are ours. They have been purchased through the precious blood of Jesus. All we have to do is confess and believe and we shall have that which has been promised to us in His Word. Mark 11:23-24 says, *"For most assuredly I tell you, if **Paul** tells this mountain, 'Be taken up and cast into the sea,' and doesn't doubt in **his** heart, but believes that what **he** says is happening; Paul shall have whatever **he** says. Therefore I tell you, all things whatever **Paul** prays and asks for, if **he** believes that **he** receives them, then **he** shall have them."* (Matt 21:20-22)[2] The prayer of faith is believing our prayer is heard before we see the answer materialized. "And this is the confidence that **Paul** has in Him, that, if **Paul** asks any thing according to His will, He hears **Paul**." (1 John 5:14) Faith refuses to see anything contrary to the Word of God.

Our prayer is as you confess these Scriptures over your life and believe what He has promised belongs to you, you will experience the fullness of His salvation: spirit, soul and body. As you do that, may you find an urgency to proclaim God's goodness and love to everyone you touch throughout your life.

Paul, it is important for you to recognize that God's promises are only for those who have given their hearts to Jesus. Whether you attend church regularly or not at all, you need to make Jesus your personal Lord and Savior for His promises to have an effect in your life. Romans 3:23 tells us: "For ***Paul*** has sinned, and ***he*** has fallen short of the glory of God." But the good news follows right after that in Romans 3:24: "But ***Paul*** is justified freely by His grace through the redemption that is in Christ Jesus."

If you have never taken this step before, ***Paul***, why not do it right now? Romans 10:9 tells us: "If ***Paul*** will confess with ***his*** mouth the Lord Jesus, and believe in ***his*** heart that God raised Him from the dead, ***Paul*** will be saved."

Just pray this prayer: *Jesus, I believe that You are the Son of God. I know that I am a sinner and I repent of all my sins. I believe that You,*

*Jesus, died for my sins and that God raised You, Jesus, from the dead. Right now, I turn from my sins and open the door of my heart to You. I receive You, Jesus, as my personal Lord and Savior. Thank you for saving me and cleansing me from all unrighteousness through Your precious blood. I thank you I am now a **son** of God. Amen.*

[1] Parallel passages in other Gospels are shown in parentheses

Finally, "May the God of peace Himself sanctify **Paul** completely. May **Paul's** whole spirit, soul, and body be preserved blameless at the coming of **Paul's** Lord, Jesus Christ." (1 Thes. 5:23)

Gill and Corinne Keith, Publishers, Personal Promise Bible® Series

The Personal Promise Bible® Series is dedicated in loving memory of Paul Keith and Amy Deyo.

please visit: www.PersonalPromiseBible.com/dedication.html

Chapter A

God's Nature

Exodus 12:23   For Yahweh will pass through to strike the Egyptians; and when He sees the blood on the lintel, and on the two doorposts, Yahweh will pass over the door, and will not allow the destroyer to come in to your houses to strike you.

Exodus 23:25-26   **Paul** shall serve Yahweh **his** God, and He (God) will bless **his** bread and **his** water, and I (God) will take sickness away from **Paul's** midst. No one will miscarry or be barren in **his** land. I will fulfill the number of **Paul's** days.

Numbers 21:8-9   Yahweh said to Moses, "Make a fiery serpent, and set it on a standard: and it shall happen, that everyone who is bitten, when he sees it, shall live." Moses made a serpent of brass, and set it on the standard: and it happened, that if a serpent had bitten any man, when he looked to the serpent of brass, he lived.

Numbers 23:19   God is not a man, that He should lie, nor the son of man, that He should repent.   Has He said, and will He not do it? Or has He spoken, and will He not make it good?

Deuteronomy 7:9   Know therefore that Yahweh ***Paul's*** God, He is God, the faithful God, who keeps covenant and loving kindness with ***Paul*** who loves Him and keeps His commandments to a thousand generations,

1 Chronicles 4:10   Jabez called on the God of Israel, saying, "Oh that You would bless ***Paul*** indeed, and enlarge ***his*** border, and that Your hand might be with ***him***, and that You would keep ***Paul*** from evil, that it not be to ***his*** sorrow!" God granted ***Paul*** that which ***he*** requested.

2 Chronicles 6:14   And he said, "Yahweh, the God of Israel, there is no God like You, in heaven, or on earth; You who keep covenant and loving kindness with ***Paul***, Your servant, who walks before You with all ***his*** heart."

2 Chronicles 7:14   If My people, who are called by My name, shall humble themselves, and pray, and seek My face, and turn from their wicked ways; then will I hear from heaven, and will forgive their sin, and will heal their land.

Nehemiah 9:21   "Yes, forty years you sustained them in the wilderness. They lacked nothing. Their clothes didn't grow old, and their feet didn't swell.
Job 36:15   Behold, God is mighty, and doesn't despise anyone. He is mighty in strength of understanding.

Psalm 9:9   The LORD will be a high tower for ***Paul*** when ***he*** is
　　　　　oppressed;
　　A high tower in times of trouble.

Psalm 25:10   All the paths of the LORD are mercy and truth for ***Paul***,

Because *he* keeps His covenant and His testimonies.

<u>Psalm 30:2</u>   O L<small>ORD</small> God, ***Paul*** cried to You, and You have healed ***him***.

<u>Psalm 34:10</u>   The young lions do lack and suffer hunger,
But if ***Paul*** seeks the L<small>ORD</small>, ***he*** shall not lack any good thing.

<u>Psalm 35:27</u>   Let them shout for joy and be glad, who favor my righteous cause.
Yes, let them say continually, "The L<small>ORD</small> be magnified,
Who has pleasure in the prosperity of His servant!"

<u>Psalm 37:4</u>   ***Paul*** is to delight ***himself*** in the L<small>ORD</small>, And He will give ***Paul*** the desires of ***his*** heart.

<u>Psalm 54:7</u>   For He has delivered ***Paul*** out of all trouble.
Paul's eyes have looked in triumph on ***his*** enemies.

<u>Psalm 84:11</u>   For the L<small>ORD</small> God is a sun and a shield. The L<small>ORD</small> will give grace and glory.
He withholds no good thing from ***Paul*** because ***he*** walks uprightly.

<u>Psalm 86:5</u>   For You, O Lord, are good, and ready to forgive ***Paul***;
Abundant in mercy toward ***Paul*** when ***he*** calls on You.

<u>Psalm 91:2-3</u>   ***Paul*** will say of the L<small>ORD</small>, "He is my refuge and my fortress;
My God, in whom I trust."
For He will deliver ***Paul*** from the snare of the fowler,
and from the deadly pestilence.

<u>Psalm 91:10-11</u>   No evil shall happen to ***Paul***,
Neither shall any plague come near ***Paul's*** dwelling.
For He will give His angels charge over ***Paul***,
To guard ***him*** in all ***his*** ways.

<u>Psalm 91:14-16</u>   "Because ***Paul*** has set ***his*** love on Me, therefore I will deliver ***him***.
I will set ***Paul*** on high, because ***he*** has known My name.
Paul will call on Me, and I will answer ***him***.
I will be with ***Paul*** in trouble.
I will deliver ***Paul***, and honor ***him***.

I will satisfy ***Paul*** with long life,
>   And show ***him*** My salvation."

Psalm 103:2-5   Praise the LORD, ***Paul's*** soul,
>   And don't forget all His benefits;
>   Who forgives all of ***Paul's*** sins; Who heals all of ***Paul's*** diseases;
Who redeems ***Paul's*** life from destruction;
>   Who crowns ***Paul*** with steadfast love and tender mercies;
Who satisfies ***Paul's*** desire with good things,
>   So that ***Paul's*** youth is renewed like the eagle's.

Psalm 105:37   He brought them forth with silver and gold.
>   There was not one feeble person among His tribes.

Psalm 107:6   Then they cried to the LORD in their trouble, And He delivered them out of their distresses.

Psalm 107:20   He sent His word, and healed ***Paul***,
>   and delivered ***him*** from the grave.

Psalm 107:41   Yet He lifts ***Paul*** out of ***his*** affliction when ***he*** is in need,
>   And increases ***Paul's*** family like a flock.

Psalm 138:2   ***Paul*** will bow down toward Your holy temple,
>   And give thanks to Your name for Your mercy and for Your truth;
>   For You have exalted Your name and Your word above all.

Psalm 145:8-9   The LORD is gracious, merciful,
>   Slow to anger, and of great mercy toward ***Paul***.
The LORD is good to ***Paul*** and to all.
>   His tender mercies are over all His works.

Psalm 147:3   He heals ***Paul's*** broken heart,
>   And binds up ***his*** wounds.

Proverbs 9:11   For by me (Wisdom) ***Paul's*** days will be multiplied.
>   The years of ***his*** life will be increased.

Isaiah 19:22   Yahweh will strike Egypt, striking and healing. They will return to Yahweh, and He will be entreated by them, and will heal them.

Isaiah 55:11   So shall My word be that goes forth out of My mouth: it shall not return to Me void, but it shall accomplish that which I please, and it shall prosper in the thing I sent it to do.

Jeremiah 17:14   Heal *Paul*, O Yahweh, and *he* shall be healed; save *Paul*, and *he* shall be saved: for You are *his* praise.

Jeremiah 29:11   For I know the thoughts that I think toward *Paul*, says Yahweh, thoughts of peace, and not of evil, to give *Paul* hope and a future.

Jeremiah 30:17a   For I will restore health to *Paul*, and I will heal *Paul* of *his* wounds, says Yahweh.

Jeremiah 33:6-7   Behold, I will bring it health and cure, and I will cure them; and I will reveal to them abundance of peace and truth. I will cause the captivity of Judah and the captivity of Israel to return, and will build them, as at the first.

Lamentations 3:22-23   It is of Yahweh's loving kindnesses that *Paul* is not consumed, because His compassion doesn't fail. They are new every morning; great is Your faithfulness.

Malachi 3:6   "For I, Yahweh, don't change; therefore you, *Paul*, are not consumed.

John 5:21   *For as the Father raises the dead and gives them life, even so the Son also gives life to* ***Paul***.

John 10:10   *The thief only comes to steal, kill, and destroy. I came that* ***Paul*** *may have life, and may have it abundantly.*

Romans 8:11   But if the Spirit of Him who raised Jesus from the dead dwells in *Paul*, He who raised Christ Jesus from the dead will also give life to *his* mortal body through His Spirit who dwells in *Paul*.

2 Corinthians 1:3-4   Blessed be the God and Father of ***Paul's*** Lord, Jesus Christ, the Father of mercies and the God of all comfort; who comforts us in all our affliction, that we may be able to comfort *Paul* in any affliction, through the comfort with which we ourselves are comforted by God.

Galatians 3:13-14   Christ redeemed *Paul* from the curse of the law, having become a curse for *him*. For it is written, "Cursed is everyone who hangs on a tree," that the blessing of Abraham might come on *Paul* through Christ Jesus; that *Paul* might receive the promise of the Spirit through faith.

Philippians 4:19   My God will supply every need of *Paul's* according to His riches in glory in Christ Jesus.

Colossians 1:13   Who delivered *Paul* out of the power of darkness, and translated *him* into the kingdom of the Son of His love;
1 Thessalonians 5:23-24   May the God of peace Himself sanctify *Paul* completely. May *Paul's* whole spirit, soul, and body be preserved blameless at the coming of *Paul's* Lord, Jesus Christ. Faithful is He who calls *Paul*, who will also do it.

2 Timothy 1:7   For God didn't give *Paul* a spirit of fear, but of power and love and self-discipline.

Hebrews 2:14-16   Since then *Paul* has shared in flesh and blood, He Himself likewise partook of the same nature, that through death He might destroy him who had the power of death, that is, the devil, and might deliver *Paul* who through fear of death was all *his* lifetime subject to bondage. For most assuredly, not to angels does He give help, but He gives help to the seed of Abraham.
Hebrews 13:8   Jesus Christ is the same yesterday, today, and forever.

1 Peter 2:10   Though in time past *Paul* was not part of a people, but now *he* is part of God's people, though *Paul* had not obtained mercy, now *he* has obtained mercy.

1 Peter 2:23-25   When He was reviled, He didn't revile back. When He suffered, He didn't threaten, but committed Himself to Him who judges righteously. He bore *Paul's* sins in His body on the tree, that *Paul*, having died to sins, might live to righteousness; by His stripes *Paul* was healed. For *Paul* was going astray like a sheep; but *he* has now returned to the Shepherd and Overseer of *his* soul.

2 Peter 3:9   Not rendering evil for evil, or reviling for reviling; but instead blessing; knowing that *Paul* was called that *he* may inherit a blessing.

James 1:17-18   Every good gift and every perfect gift is from above, coming down from the Father of lights, with whom can be no variation, nor shifting shadow. Of His own will He brought *Paul* forth by the word of truth, that *Paul* should be a kind of first fruit of His creatures.

James 5:11   We call them blessed who endured. You have heard of the patience of Job, and have seen the purpose of the Lord, and how the Lord is full of compassion and mercy.

1 John 3:8   He who sins is of the devil, for the devil has been sinning from the beginning. To this end the Son of God was revealed, that He might destroy the works of the devil.

Chapter B

Salvation for *Paul*

Psalm 37:39-40   But *Paul's* salvation, because *he* is righteous, is from
      the LORD.
   He is *Paul's* stronghold in the time of trouble.
   The LORD helps *Paul*, and rescues *him*.
He rescues *Paul* from the wicked, and saves *him*,
   Because *Paul* has taken refuge in Him.

Psalm 68:19   Blessed be the Lord, who daily bears *Paul's* burdens,
   Even the God who is *Paul's* salvation.
   Selah.

Psalm 118:14   The LORD is *Paul's* strength and song.
   He has become *Paul's* salvation.

Psalm 119:45 *Paul* will walk in liberty,
For *he* has sought Your precepts.
Isaiah 12:2-3 Behold, God is *Paul's* salvation. *He* will trust, and will not be afraid; for Yah, Yahweh, is *his* strength and song; and He has become *Paul's* salvation." Therefore with joy *Paul* will draw water out of the wells of salvation.

John 3:17 *For God didn't send His Son into the world to judge Paul, but that Paul should be saved through Him.*

John 10:9-10 *I am the door. If Paul enters in by Me, he will be saved, and will go in and go out, and will find pasture. The thief only comes to steal, kill, and destroy. I came that Paul may have life, and may have it abundantly.*

Acts 2:21 It will be, that whoever will call on the name of the Lord will be saved.
Acts 4:12 There is salvation in none other, for neither is there any other name under heaven, that is given among men, by which we must be saved!

Romans 1:16 For I am not ashamed of the gospel of Christ, for it is the power of God to salvation for everyone who believes; first for the Jew, but also for *Paul*.

Romans 10:9-10 That if *Paul* will confess with *his* mouth the Lord Jesus, and believe in *his* heart that God raised Him from the dead, *Paul* will be saved. For with the heart, *Paul* believes unto righteousness; and with *his* mouth confession is made unto salvation.

1 Corinthians 1:20-21 Where are the wise? Where is the scribe? Where is the lawyer of this world? Hasn't God made foolish the wisdom of this world? For in the wisdom of God, the world through its wisdom didn't know God. It pleased God through the foolishness of the preaching to save *Paul* because *he* believes.

Ephesians 2:4-5 But God, being rich in mercy, for His great love with which He loved *Paul*, even when *he* was dead in *his* trespasses, made *him* alive together with Christ (by grace *Paul* has been saved).

Ephesians 2:8-9   For by grace *Paul* has been saved through faith, and that not of *himself*; it is the gift of God, not of works, so that *Paul* cannot boast.

Titus 3:4-5   But when the kindness of God *Paul's* Savior and His love toward *Paul* appeared, not by works of righteousness, which *Paul* did *himself*, but according to His mercy, He saved *Paul*, through the washing of regeneration and renewing by the Holy Spirit.

Hebrews 10:39   But *Paul* is not of those who shrink back to destruction, but *he* is of those who have faith to the saving of *his* soul.

James 1:21   Therefore, putting away all filthiness and overflowing of wickedness, *Paul* should receive with humility the implanted word, which is able to save *his* soul.

Chapter C

Jesus' Miracles

Matthew 8:2-3   Behold, a leper came to Him and worshipped Him, saying, "Lord, if You want to, You can make me clean." Jesus stretched out His hand, and touched him, saying, *"I want to. Be made clean."* Immediately his leprosy was cleansed. (Mk 1:40-45; Lk 5:12-16)

Matthew 8:14-15   When Jesus came into Peter's house, He saw his wife's mother lying sick with a fever. He touched her hand, and the fever left her. She got up and served Him. (Mk 1:29-34; Lk 4:38-39)

Matthew 11:4-5   Jesus answered them, *"Go and tell John the things which you hear and see: the blind receive their sight, the lame walk, the lepers are cleansed, the deaf hear, the dead are raised up, and the poor have good news preached to them.*(Lk 7:21-23)

Matthew 12:22-29   Then one possessed by a demon, blind and mute, was brought to Him and He healed him, so that the blind and mute man both spoke and saw. All the multitudes were amazed, and said, "Can this be the Son of David?" But when the Pharisees heard it, they said, "This man does not cast out demons, except by Beelzebul, the prince of the demons." Knowing their thoughts, Jesus said to them, *"Every kingdom divided against itself is brought to desolation, and every city or house divided against itself will not stand. If Satan casts out Satan, he is divided against himself. How then will his kingdom stand? If I by Beelzebul cast out demons, by whom do your sons cast them out? Therefore they will be your judges. But if I by the Spirit of God cast out demons, then the kingdom of God has come upon you. Or how can* **Paul** *enter into the house of the strong man, and plunder his goods, unless someone first binds the strong man? Then he will plunder the strong man's house.* (Lk 11:14-23)

Matthew 14:14   Jesus went out, and He saw a great multitude. He had compassion on them, and healed their sick.   (Mk 6:34; Lk 9:11; John 6:2)

Matthew 15:22-28   Behold, a Canaanite woman came out from those borders, and cried, saying, "Have mercy on me, O Lord, Son of David! My daughter is severely demonized!" But He answered her not a word. His disciples came and begged Him, saying, "Send her away; for she cries after us." But He answered, *"I wasn't sent to anyone but the lost sheep of the house of Israel."* But she came and worshipped Him, saying, "Lord, help me." But He answered, *"It is not appropriate to take the children's bread and throw it to the dogs."* But she said, "Yes, Lord, but even the dogs eat the crumbs which fall from their masters' table." Then Jesus answered her, *"Woman, great is your faith! Be it done to you even as you desire."* And her daughter was healed from that hour.   (Mk 7:24-30)

Matthew 15:29-31   Jesus departed there, and came near to the Sea of Galilee; and He went up into the mountain, and sat there. Great multitudes came to Him, having with them the lame, blind, mute, maimed, and many others, and they put them down at Jesus' feet. He healed them, so that the multitude wondered when they saw the mute speaking, injured whole, lame walking, and blind seeing — and they glorified the God of Israel.   (Mk 7:31-37)

Matthew 19:1-2   It happened when Jesus had finished these words, He departed from Galilee, and came into the borders of Judea beyond the

Jordan. Great multitudes followed Him, and He healed them there. (Lk 9:51-56; John 7:10)

Matthew 20:29-34   As they went out from Jericho, a great multitude followed Him. Behold, two blind men sitting by the road, when they heard that Jesus was passing by, cried out, "Lord, have mercy on us, Son of David!" The multitude rebuked them, telling them that they should be quiet, but they cried out even more, "Lord, have mercy on us, Son of David!" Jesus stood still, and called them, and asked, *"What do you want Me to do for you?"* They told Him, "Lord, that our eyes may be opened." Jesus, being moved with compassion, touched their eyes; and immediately their eyes received their sight, and they followed Him. (Matt 21:14-15)

Mark 1:32-34   At evening, when the sun had set, they brought to Him all who were sick, and those who were possessed by demons. All the city was gathered together at the door. He healed many who were sick with various diseases, and cast out many demons. He didn't allow the demons to speak, because they knew Him.   (Matt 8:14; Lk 4:38-41)

Mark 2:1-12   When He entered into Capernaum again after several days, it was heard that He was in the house. Immediately many were gathered together, so that there was no more room, not even around the door; and He spoke the word to them. Four people came, carrying a paralytic to Him. When they could not come near to Him for the crowd, they removed the roof where He was. When they had broken it up, they let down the mat that the paralytic was lying on. Jesus, seeing their faith, said to the paralytic, *"Son, your sins are forgiven you."* But there were some of the scribes sitting there, and reasoning in their hearts, "Why does this Man speak blasphemies like that? Who can forgive sins but God alone?" Immediately Jesus, perceiving in His spirit that they so reasoned within themselves, said to them, *"Why do you reason these things in your hearts? Which is easier, to tell the paralytic, 'Your sins are forgiven;' or to say, 'Arise, and take up your bed, and walk?' But that you may know that the Son of Man has authority on earth to forgive sins"* — He said to the paralytic — *"I tell you, arise, take up your mat, and go to your house."* He arose, and immediately took up the mat, and went out in front of them all. They were all amazed, and glorified God, saying, "We have never seen anything like this!" (Matt 9:1-8; Lk 5:17-26)

Mark 3:1-6   He entered again into the synagogue, and there was a man there whose hand was withered. They watched Him, whether He would heal him on the Sabbath day, that they might accuse Him. He said to the man whose hand was withered, *"Stand up." He said to them, "Is it lawful on the Sabbath day to do good, or to do harm? To save a life, or to kill?"* But they were silent. When He had looked around at them with anger, being grieved at the hardening of their hearts, He said to the man, *"Stretch out your hand."* He stretched it out, and his hand was restored as healthy as the other. The Pharisees went out, and immediately conspired with the Herodians against Him, how they might destroy Him. (Matt 12:9-14; Lk 6:6-11)

Mark 5:21-43   When Jesus had crossed back over in the boat to the other side, a great multitude was gathered to Him; and He was by the sea. Behold, one of the rulers of the synagogue, Jairus by name, came; and seeing Him, he fell at His feet, and begged Him earnestly, saying, "My little daughter is at the point of death. Please come and lay Your hands on her, that she may be made healthy, and live."

He went with him, and a great multitude followed Him, and they pressed upon Him on all sides. A certain woman, who had an issue of blood for twelve years, and had suffered many things by many physicians, and had spent all that she had, and was no better, but rather grew worse, having heard the things concerning Jesus, came up behind Him in the crowd, and touched His clothes. For she said, "If I just touch His clothes, I will be made well." Immediately the flow of her blood was dried up, and she felt in her body that she was healed of her affliction.

Immediately Jesus, perceiving in Himself that the power had gone out from Him, turned around in the crowd, and asked, *"Who touched My clothes?"*

His disciples said to Him, "You see the multitude pressing against You, and You say, 'Who touched Me?'"

He looked around to see her who had done this thing. But the woman, fearing and trembling, knowing what had been done to her, came and fell down before Him, and told Him all the truth.

He said to her, *"Daughter, your faith has made you well. Go in peace, and be cured of your disease."*

While He was still speaking, they came from the synagogue ruler's house saying, "Your daughter is dead. Why bother the Teacher any more?"

But Jesus, when He heard the message spoken, immediately said to the ruler of the synagogue, *"Don't be afraid, only believe."* He allowed no one to follow Him, except Peter, James, and John the brother of James. He came to the synagogue ruler's house, and He saw an uproar, weeping, and great wailing. When He had entered in, He said to them, *"Why do you make an uproar and weep? The child is not dead, but is asleep."*

They ridiculed Him. But He, having put them all out, took the father of the child and her mother and those who were with Him, and went in where the child was lying. Taking the child by the hand, He said to her, *"Talitha cumi;"* which means, being interpreted, *"Girl, I tell you, get up."* Immediately the girl rose up, and walked, for she was twelve years old. They were overcome with great amazement. He strictly ordered them that no one should know this, and commanded that something should be given to her to eat. (Matt 9:18-26; Lk 8:40-56)

Mark 6:5   He could do no mighty work there, except that He laid His hands on a few sick folk, and healed them. (Matt 13:53-58)

Mark 7:32-35   They brought to Him one who was deaf and had an impediment in his speech. They begged Him to lay His hand on him. He took him aside from the multitude, privately, and put His fingers into his ears, and He spat, and touched his tongue. Looking up to heaven, He sighed, and said to him, *"Ephphatha!"* that is, *"Be opened!"* Immediately his ears were opened, and the impediment of his tongue was released, and he spoke clearly. (Matt 15:29-31)

Mark 8:22-25   He came to Bethsaida. They brought a blind man to Him, and begged Him to touch him. He took hold of the blind man by the hand, and brought him out of the village. When He had spit on his eyes, and laid His hands on him, He asked him if he saw anything. He looked up, and said, "I see men; for I see them like trees walking." Then again He laid His hands on his eyes. He looked intently, and was restored, and saw everyone clearly. He sent him away to his house, saying, *"Don't enter into the village, nor tell anyone in the village."*

Mark 9:17-27   One of the multitude answered, "Teacher, I brought to You my son, who has a mute spirit; and wherever it seizes him, it throws him down, and he foams at the mouth, and grinds his teeth, and wastes away. I asked Your disciples to cast it out, and they weren't able."

He answered him, *"Unbelieving generation, how long shall I be with you? How long shall I bear with you? Bring him to Me."*

They brought him to Him, and when he saw Him, immediately the spirit convulsed him, and he fell on the ground, wallowing and foaming at the mouth.

He asked his father, *"How long has this been happening to him?"*

He said, "From childhood. Often it has cast him both into the fire and into the water, to destroy him. But if You can do anything, have compassion on us, and help us."

*"If **Paul** can believe,"* Jesus said to him, *"all things are possible to **Paul** if **he** believes."*

Immediately the father of the child cried out with tears, "I believe. Help my unbelief!"

When Jesus saw that a multitude came running together, He rebuked the unclean spirit, saying to him, *"You mute and deaf spirit, I command you, come out of him, and never enter him again!"*

Having cried out, and convulsing him greatly, it came out of him. The boy became like one dead; so much that most of them said, "He is dead."

But Jesus took him by the hand, and raised him up; and he arose. (Matt 17:14-21; Lk 9:37-42)

Luke 4:16-19   He came to Nazareth, where He had been brought up. He entered, as was His custom, into the synagogue on the Sabbath day, and stood up to read. The book of the prophet Isaiah was handed to Him. He opened the book, and found the place where it was written,

> *"The Spirit of the Lord is on Me,*
> *   Because He has anointed Me to preach good news to **Paul**.*
> *He has sent Me to heal **Paul** when **he** is brokenhearted,*
> *   To proclaim release to **Paul** when **he** is held captive,*
> *   Recovery of sight for **Paul** when **he** is blind,*
> *   To deliver **Paul** when **he** is crushed,*
> *   And to proclaim the acceptable year of the Lord."*

Luke 4:32-36   And they were astonished at His teaching, for His word was with authority. In the synagogue there was a man who had a spirit of an unclean demon, and he cried out with a loud voice, saying, "Ah! what have we to do with You, Jesus of Nazareth? Have You come to destroy us? I know who You are: the Holy One of God!"

Jesus rebuked him, saying, *"Be silent, and come out of him!"* When the demon had thrown him down in their midst, he came out of him, having done him no harm.

Amazement came on all, and they spoke together, one with another, saying, "What is this word? For with authority and power He commands the unclean spirits, and they come out!" (Mk 1:23-28)

Luke 5:12-13   It happened, while He was in one of the cities, behold, there was a man full of leprosy. When he saw Jesus, he fell on his face, and begged Him, saying, "Lord, if You want to, You can make me clean." He stretched out His hand, and touched him, saying, *"I want to. Be made clean."* Immediately the leprosy left him.

Luke 5:17-25   It happened on one of those days, that He was teaching; and there were Pharisees and teachers of the law sitting by, who had come out of every village of Galilee, Judea, and Jerusalem. The power of the Lord was with Him to heal them. Behold, men brought a paralyzed man on a cot, and they sought to bring him in to lay before Jesus. Not finding a way to bring him in because of the multitude, they went up to the roof, and let him down through the tiles with his cot into the midst before Jesus. Seeing their faith, He said to him, *"Man, your sins are forgiven you."*

The scribes and the Pharisees began to reason, saying, "Who is this that speaks blasphemies? Who can forgive sins, but God alone?"

But Jesus, perceiving their thoughts, answered them, *"Why are you reasoning so in your hearts? Which is easier to say, 'Your sins are forgiven you;' or to say, 'Arise and walk?' But that you may know that the Son of Man has authority on earth to forgive sins"* (He said to the paralyzed man), *"I tell you, arise, and take up your cot, and go to your house."* Immediately he rose up before them, and took up that which he was laying on, and departed to his house, glorifying God. (Matt 9:1-8; Mk 2:8-12)

Luke 6:6-11   It also happened on another Sabbath that He entered into the synagogue and taught. There was a man there, and his right hand was withered. The scribes and the Pharisees watched Him, to see whether He would heal on the Sabbath, that they might find an accusation against Him. But He knew their thoughts; and He said to the man who had the withered hand, *"Rise up, and stand in the middle."* He arose and stood. Then Jesus said to them, *"I will ask you something: Is it lawful on the Sabbath to do good, or to do harm? To save a life, or to kill?"* He looked around at all of them, and said to the man, *"Stretch out your hand."* He did, and his hand was restored as sound as the other. But they were filled with rage, and talked with one another about what they might do to Jesus. (Matt 12:9; Mk 3:1-6)

Luke 7:2-10   A certain centurion's servant, who was dear to him, was sick and at the point of death. When he heard about Jesus, he sent to Him elders of the Jews, asking Him to come and save his servant. When they came to Jesus, they begged Him earnestly, saying, "He is worthy for you to do this for him, for he loves our nation, and he built our synagogue for us." Jesus went with them. When He was not far from the house, the centurion sent friends to Him, saying to Him, "Lord, don't trouble Yourself, for I am not worthy for You to come under my roof. Therefore I didn't even think myself worthy to come to You; but say the word, and my servant will be healed. For I also am a man placed under authority, having under myself soldiers. I tell this one, 'Go!' and he goes; and to another, 'Come!' and he comes; and to my servant, 'Do this,' and he does it."

When Jesus heard these things, He marveled at him, and turned and said to the multitude who followed Him, *"I tell you, I have not found such great faith, no, not in Israel."* Those who were sent, returning to the house, found that the servant who had been sick was well. (Matt 8:5-13)

Luke 7:11-15 It happened soon afterwards, that He went to a city called Nain. Many of His disciples, along with a great multitude, went with Him. Now when He drew near to the gate of the city, behold, one who was dead was carried out, the only son of his mother, and she was a widow. Many people of the city were with her. When the Lord saw her, He had compassion on her, and said to her, *"Don't cry."* He came near and touched the coffin, and the bearers stood still. He said, *"Young man, I tell you, arise!"* He who was dead sat up, and began to speak. And He gave him to his mother.

Luke 7:21 In that hour He cured many of diseases and plagues and evil spirits; and to many who were blind He gave sight. (Matt 11:2-19)

Luke 8:35-36 People went out to see what had happened. They came to Jesus, and found the man from whom the demons had gone out, sitting at Jesus' feet, clothed and in his right mind; and they were afraid. Those who saw it told them how he who had been possessed by demons was healed. (Matt 8:28-34; Mk5:1-20)

Luke 8:49-50 While He still spoke, one from the ruler of the synagogue's house came, saying to him, "Your daughter is dead. Don't trouble the Teacher." But Jesus hearing it, answered him, *"Don't be afraid. Only believe, and she will be healed."*

Luke 9:11   But the multitudes, perceiving it, followed Him. He welcomed them, and spoke to them of the kingdom of God, and He cured those who needed healing.

Luke 11:14   He was casting out a demon that was mute. It happened, when the demon had gone out, the mute man spoke; and the multitudes marveled. (Matt 12:22-37; Mk 3:20-30)

Luke 13:10-13   When Jesus saw her, He called her, and said to her, *"Woman, you are freed from your infirmity."* He laid His hands on her, and immediately she stood up straight, and glorified God.

Luke 22:50-51   A certain one of them struck the servant of the high priest, and cut off his right ear. But Jesus answered, *"Let Me at least do this"* — and He touched his ear, and healed him.

John 5:2-9   Now in Jerusalem by the sheep gate, there is a pool, which is called in Hebrew, "Bethesda," having five porches. In these lay a great multitude of those who were sick, blind, lame, or paralyzed, waiting for the moving of the water; for an angel of the Lord went down at certain times into the pool, and stirred up the water. Whoever stepped in first after the stirring of the water was made whole of whatever disease they had. A certain man was there, who had been sick for thirty-eight years. When Jesus saw him lying there, and knew that he had been sick for a long time, He asked him, *"Do you want to be made well?"* The sick man answered Him, "Sir, I have no one to put me into the pool when the water is stirred up, but while I'm coming, another steps down before me." Jesus said to him, *"Arise, take up your mat, and walk."* Immediately, the man was made well, and took up his mat and walked. Now it was the Sabbath on that day.

John 9:1-7   As he passed by, He saw a man blind from birth. His disciples asked Him, "Teacher, who sinned, this man or his parents, that he was born blind?" Jesus answered, *"Neither did this man sin, nor his parents; but, that the works of God might be revealed in him. I must work the works of Him who sent Me, while it is day. The night is coming, when no one can work. While I am in the world, I am the light of the world."*

When He had said this, He spat on the ground, made mud with the saliva, anointed the blind man's eyes with the mud, and said to him, *"Go, wash in the pool of Siloam"* (which means "Sent"). So he went away, washed, and came back seeing.

<u>John 9:32-33</u> Since the world began it has never been heard of that anyone opened the eyes of someone born blind. If this Man were not from God, He could do nothing."

<u>John 10:37-38</u> *If I don't do the works of My Father, don't believe Me. But if I do them, though you don't believe Me, believe the works; that you may know and believe that the Father is in Me, and I in the Father."*

<u>John 11:34-44</u> and said, *"Where have you laid him?"* They told Him, "Lord, come and see." Jesus wept. The Jews therefore said, "See how much affection He had for him!" Some of them said, "Couldn't this Man, who opened the eyes of him who was blind, have also kept this man from dying?" Jesus, again groaning in Himself, came to the tomb. Now it was a cave, and a stone lay against it. Jesus said, *"Take away the stone."* Martha, the sister of him who was dead, said to Him, "Lord, by this time there is a stench, for he has been dead four days." Jesus said to her, *"Didn't I tell you that if you believed, you would see God's glory?"* So they took away the stone from the place where the dead man was lying. Jesus lifted up His eyes, and said, *"Father, I thank You that You listened to Me. I know that You always listen to Me, but because of the multitude that stands around I said this, that they may believe that You sent Me."* When He had said this, He cried with a loud voice, *"Lazarus, come out!"* He who was dead came out, bound hand and foot with wrappings, and his face was wrapped around with a cloth. Jesus said to them, *"Free him, and let him go."*

<u>Acts 10:38-39</u> Even Jesus of Nazareth, how God anointed Him with the Holy Spirit and with power, who went about doing good and healing all who were oppressed by the devil, for God was with Him. We are witnesses of everything He did both in the country of the Jews, and in Jerusalem; whom they killed, hanging Him on a tree.

Chapter D

Jesus Healed All

Matthew 4:23-24   Jesus went about in all Galilee, teaching in their synagogues, preaching the gospel of the kingdom, and healing every disease and every sickness among the people. The report about Him went out into all Syria. They brought to Him all who were sick, afflicted with various diseases and torments, possessed with demons, epileptics, and paralytics; and He healed them. (Mk. 1:35-39; Lk 4:42-44)

Matthew 8:16-17   When evening came, they brought to Him many possessed with demons. He cast out the spirits with a word, and healed all who were sick; that it might be fulfilled which was spoken through Isaiah the prophet, saying: "He took ***Paul's*** infirmities, and bore ***Paul's*** diseases." (Mk 1:32; Lk 4:40)

Matthew 9:32-35   As they went out, behold, a mute man who was demon possessed was brought to Him. When the demon was cast out, the mute man spoke. The multitudes marveled, saying, "Nothing like this has ever been seen in Israel!" But the Pharisees said, "By the prince of the demons, He casts out demons." Jesus went about all the cities and the villages, teaching in their synagogues, and preaching the gospel of the kingdom, and healing every disease and every sickness among the people.

Matthew 12:14-15   But the Pharisees went out, and conspired against Him, how they might destroy Him. Jesus, perceiving that, withdrew from there. Great multitudes followed Him; and He healed them all, (Mk 3:1-6; Lk 6:6-11)

Matthew 14:34-36   When they had crossed over, they came to the land of Gennesaret. When the men of that place recognized Him, they sent into all that surrounding region, and brought to Him all who were sick, and they begged Him that they might just touch the fringe of His garment. As many as touched it were made whole. (Mk 6:53-56)

Luke 6:17-19   He came down with them, and stood on a level place, with a crowd of His disciples, and a great number of the people from all Judea and Jerusalem, and the sea coast of Tyre and Sidon, who came to hear Him and to be healed of their diseases; as well as those who were troubled by unclean spirits, and they were healed. All the multitude sought to touch Him, for power came out from Him and healed them all. (Matt 12:15; Mk 3:10)

Acts 5:16   Multitudes also came together from the cities around Jerusalem, bringing sick people, and those who were tormented by unclean spirits: and they were all healed.

Chapter E

Paul's **Part in Wholeness**

Exodus 15:26   And he said, "If you will diligently listen to the voice of Yahweh *Paul's* God, and will do that which is right in His eyes, and will pay attention to His commandments, and keep all His statutes, I will put none of the diseases on you, which I have put on the Egyptians; for I am Yahweh who heals *Paul*."

Deuteronomy 7:11-16   *Paul* shall therefore keep the commandment, and the statutes, and the ordinances, which I command *him* this day, to do them. It shall happen, because *Paul* listens to these ordinances, and keeps and does them, that Yahweh *Paul's* God will keep with *him* the covenant and the loving kindness which He swore to *Paul's* fathers: and He will love *Paul*, and bless *Paul*, and multiply *Paul*; He will also bless the fruit of *his* body and the fruit of *his* ground, *his* grain and *his* new wine and *his* oil, the increase of *his* livestock and the young of *his* flock, in the land which He swore to *Paul's* fathers to give *him*. *Paul* shall be blessed above all peoples: there shall not be male or female barren with *Paul*, or among *his* livestock. Yahweh will take away from *Paul* all sickness; and none of the evil diseases of Egypt, which *Paul* knows, He will put on *him*, but will lay them on all those who hate *Paul*. *Paul* shall consume all the peoples whom Yahweh *his* God shall deliver to him; *Paul's* eye shall not pity them: neither shall *Paul* serve their gods; for that will be a snare to *Paul*.

2 Chronicles 20:21-22   When he had taken counsel with the people, he appointed those who should sing to Yahweh, and give praise in holy array, as they went out before the army, and say, "Give thanks, *Paul*, to Yahweh; for His loving kindness endures forever." When they began to sing and to praise, Yahweh set ambushers against the children of Ammon, Moab, and Mount Seir, who had come against Judah; and they were struck.

Psalm 22:4-5   Our fathers trusted in You.
    They trusted, and You delivered them.
They cried to You, and were delivered.
    They trusted in You, and were not disappointed.

Psalm 50:15   If *Paul* calls on Me in the day of trouble,
    I will deliver *Paul*, and *he* will honor Me.

Proverbs 1:33   But if *Paul* listens to me, *he* will dwell securely,
    And *he* will be at ease, without fear of harm."

Proverbs 3:1-2   My *son Paul* must not forget my teaching;
    But *his* heart must keep my commandments:
For length of days, and years of life,
    And peace, they will add to *him*.

Proverbs 3:7-8   *Paul* must not be wise in *his* own eyes.
    Paul is to fear the LORD, and depart from evil.
For it will be health to *Paul's* body,
    And nourishment to *his* bones.

Proverbs 3:16   Length of days is in her (Wisdom's) right hand.
    In her left hand are riches and honor.

Proverbs 4:6   If *Paul* does not forsake wisdom, she will preserve *him*.
    If *Paul* loves wisdom, she will keep *him*.

Proverbs 4:20-22   My *son Paul* should attend to my words.
    Paul should turn *his* ear to my sayings.

Paul should not let them depart from ***his*** eyes,
   But ***he*** is to keep them in the midst of ***his*** heart.
For they are life for ***Paul*** if ***he*** finds them,
   And health to ***his*** whole body.

Proverbs 10:27   The fear of the LORD prolongs ***Paul's*** days,
   But the years of the wicked shall be shortened.

Proverbs 12:18   There is one who speaks rashly like the piercing of a sword,
   But ***Paul*** is wise and ***his*** tongue heals.

Proverbs 14:30   A heart at peace is life for ***Paul***,
   But envy rots ***his*** bones.

Proverbs 15:4   ***Paul's*** gentle tongue is a tree of life,
   But the deceitful tongue crushes the spirit.

Proverbs 17:22   A cheerful heart is good medicine for ***Paul***,
   But a crushed spirit dries up ***his*** bones.

Proverbs 18:10   The name of the LORD is a strong tower;
   Paul, being righteous, runs to Him, and is safe.

Proverbs 28:16   A tyrannical ruler lacks judgment.
   One who hates ill-gotten gain will have long days.

Isaiah 26:3-4   You will keep ***Paul's*** mind in perfect peace, because ***he*** is steadfast, because ***he*** trusts in You. Trust in Yahweh forever, ***Paul***; for in Yahweh is an everlasting Rock.

Jonah 2:9   But ***Paul*** will sacrifice to You with the voice of thanksgiving. ***Paul*** will pay that which ***he*** has vowed. Salvation belongs to Yahweh.

Malachi 4:2   But to ***Paul***, because ***he*** fears My name, shall the sun of righteousness arise with healing in its wings. ***Paul*** will go out, and leap like a calf of the stall.

Matthew 6:33   But ***Paul*** is to seek first God's kingdom, and His righteousness; and all these things will be given to ***Paul*** as well.

Mark 9:24   Immediately the father of the child cried out with tears, "I believe. Help my unbelief!" (Matt. 16:21-26; Mark 8:31-38)

Mark 16:17-18   *These signs will accompany **Paul**: in My name **he** will cast out demons; **he** will speak with new languages; **Paul** will take up serpents; and if **he** drinks any deadly thing, it will in no way hurt **him**; **Paul** will lay **his** hands on the sick, and they will recover."*

Luke 4:18   *"The Spirit of the Lord is on Me, because He has anointed Me to preach good news to **Paul**. He has sent Me to heal **Paul** when **he** is brokenhearted, to proclaim release to **Paul** when **he** is held captive, recovery of sight for **Paul** when **he** is blind, to deliver **Paul** when **he** is crushed,*

Luke 9:1-2   He called the twelve together, and gave them power and authority over all demons, and to cure diseases. He sent them forth to preach the kingdom of God, and to heal the sick. (Matt. 10:1; Mk 6:7)

Luke 9:6   They departed, and went throughout the villages, preaching the gospel, and healing everywhere.

Luke 10:8-9   *Into whatever city you enter, and they receive you, eat the things that are set before you. Heal the sick who are therein, and tell them, 'The kingdom of God has come near to you.'*
Luke 10:19   *Behold, I give **Paul** authority to tread on serpents and scorpions, and over all the power of the enemy. Nothing will in any way hurt **Paul**.*

Acts 8:5-8   Philip went down to the city of Samaria, and proclaimed to them the Christ. The multitudes listened with one accord to the things that were spoken by Philip, when they heard and saw the signs which he did. For unclean spirits came out of many of those who had them. They came out, crying with a loud voice. Many who had been paralyzed and lame were healed. There was great joy in that city.

Acts 19:11   God worked special miracles by the hands of Paul. So that even handkerchiefs or aprons were carried away from his body to the sick, and the evil spirits went out.

Acts 28:8-9   It happened that the father of Publius lay sick with fever and dysentery. Paul went to him, prayed, and laying his hands on him, healed him. Then when this was done, the rest who had diseases on the island came and were cured.

Romans 4:19   Without being weakened in faith, he didn't consider his own body, already having been worn out, (he being about a hundred years old), and the deadness of Sarah's womb. Yet, looking to the promise of God, he didn't waver through unbelief, but grew strong through faith, giving glory to God, and being fully assured that what He had promised, He was able also to perform.

Romans 12:1-2   Therefore I urge **Paul**, by the mercies of God, to present **his** body as a living sacrifice, holy and acceptable to God, which is **Paul's** spiritual service. **Paul** is not to be conformed to this world, but is to be transformed by the renewing of **his** mind, so that **Paul** may prove what is the good, acceptable and perfect will of God.

1 Corinthians 6:20   For **Paul** was bought with a price. Therefore **Paul** is to glorify God in **his** body and in **his** spirit, which are God's.

1 Corinthians 11:29-30   For **he** who eats and drinks in an unworthy manner eats and drinks judgment to **himself**, if **he** doesn't discern the Lord's body. For this cause many among you are weak and sickly, and many sleep.

2 Corinthians 4:18   While **Paul** doesn't look at the things which **he** sees, but at the things which **he** doesn't see. For the things which **Paul** sees are temporal, but the things which **Paul** does not see are eternal.

2 Corinthians 10:4-5   For the weapons of **Paul's** warfare are not of the flesh, but mighty before God to the throwing down of strongholds, throwing down imaginations and every high thing that is exalted against the knowledge of God, and bringing every thought into captivity to the obedience of Christ;

Ephesians 4:27   Neither is **Paul** to give place to the devil.

Ephesians 4:29   Let no corrupt speech proceed out of **Paul's** mouth, but such as is good for building up according to the needs of those who hear, that it may give them grace.

Ephesians 6:11-16   **Paul** is to put on the whole armor of God that **he** may be able to stand against the wiles of the devil. For **Paul's** wrestling is not against flesh and blood, but against the principalities, against the powers, against the rulers of the darkness of this age, and against the spiritual hosts of wickedness in the heavenly places. Therefore, **Paul** should put on the whole armor of God, that **he** may be able to withstand in the evil day, and, having done all, to stand. **Paul** must stand therefore, having the belt of truth buckled around **his** waist, and having put on the breastplate of righteousness, and having fitted **his** feet with the preparation of the gospel of peace; above all, taking up the shield of faith, with which **Paul** will be able to quench all the fiery darts of the evil one.

Philippians 4:6   **Paul** is not to be anxious in anything, but in everything, by prayer and petition with thanksgiving, **Paul** is to let **his** requests be made known to God.

1 Thessalonians 2:13   For this cause we also thank God without ceasing, that, when **Paul** received the word of God, **he** accepted it not as the word of men, but, as it is in truth, the word of God, which also works in **Paul** because **he** believes.

2 Thessalonians 3:3   But the Lord is faithful, who will establish **Paul**, and guard **Paul** from the evil one.

2 Timothy 4:7   **Paul** has fought the good fight. **Paul** has finished the course. **Paul** has kept the faith.

Hebrews 3:14   For **Paul** has become a partaker of Christ, if **Paul** holds fast **his** first confidence firm to the end.

Hebrews 6:11-12   We desire that **Paul** may show diligence to the fullness of hope even to the end, that **he** won't be sluggish, but an imitator of those who through faith and patience inherited the promises.

Hebrews 10:35-36   Therefore, **Paul** must not throw away **his** boldness, which has a great reward. For **Paul** needs patience so that, having done the will of God, **he** may receive the promise.

Hebrews 11:1   Now faith is assurance of things **Paul** hopes for, proof of things **Paul** has not seen.

Hebrews 11:6   Without faith it is impossible for **Paul** to please Him, for when **Paul** comes to God, **he** must believe that He exists, and that He will reward **Paul** if **he** seeks Him.

Hebrews 13:15   Through Him let **Paul** offer up a sacrifice of praise to God continually, that is, the fruit of **his** lips which confesses His name.

James 2:18   **Paul** may say, "You have faith, and I have works." **Paul** can show me **his** faith by **his** works, and I by my works will show **Paul** my faith.

James 4:7   **Paul** must subject **himself** therefore to God. If **Paul** resists the devil, he will flee from **him**.

James 5:14-16   If **Paul** is sick, **he** should call for the elders of the church, and let them pray over **him**, anointing **him** with oil in the name of the Lord, and the prayer of faith will heal **Paul** when **he** is sick, and the Lord will raise **him** up. If **Paul** has committed sins, **he** will be forgiven. If **Paul** confesses **his** offenses to others, and prays with others, then **Paul** will be healed. The earnest prayer of a righteous **man** like **Paul** is powerful and effective.

1 Peter 5:5-6   Likewise, **Paul** must be subject to **his** elders. Yes, **Paul** is to gird **himself** with humility, to subject **himself** to others; for "God resists the proud, but gives grace to the humble." **Paul** is to humble **himself** therefore under the mighty hand of God, that He may exalt **Paul** in due time;

1 John 5:18   We know that **Paul** is born of God and doesn't sin, but because **Paul** was born of God, **he** keeps **himself** safe, and the evil one can't touch **Paul**.

<u>3 John 2</u>   I pray that ***Paul*** may prosper in all things and be in good health, even as ***his*** soul prospers.

<u>Revelation 3:11</u>   *I am coming quickly! Hold firmly that which you have, so that no one takes your crown.*

Chapter F

God's Work

    <u>2 Kings 5:10-14</u>   Elisha sent a messenger to him, saying, "Go and wash in the Jordan seven times, and your flesh shall come again to you, and you shall be clean." But Naaman was angry, and went away, and said, "Behold, I thought, 'He will surely come out to me, and stand, and call on the name of Yahweh his God, and wave his hand over the place, and heal the leper.' Aren't Abanah and Pharpar, the rivers of Damascus, better than all the waters of Israel? Couldn't I wash in them, and be clean?" So he turned and went away in a rage. His servants came near, and spoke to him, and said, "My father, if the prophet had asked you do some great thing, wouldn't you have done it? How much rather then, when he says to you, 'Wash, and be clean?'" Then went he down, and dipped *himself* seven times in the Jordan, according to the saying of the man of God; and his flesh was restored like the flesh of a little child, and he was clean.

    <u>Ruth 4:15</u>   He shall be to you a restorer of life, and sustain you in your old age, for your daughter-in-law, who loves you, who is better to you than seven sons, has borne him."

<u>Psalm 34:7</u>   The angel of the LORD encamps round about ***Paul*** because
      he fears Him, and delivers ***him***.

<u>Psalm 41:1-2</u>   Blessed is ***Paul*** if ***he*** considers the poor:
    The LORD will deliver ***Paul*** in the day of evil.
The LORD will preserve ***Paul***, and keep ***him*** alive,
    Paul shall be blessed on the earth,

And He will not surrender ***Paul*** to the will of ***his*** enemies.

Psalm 56:13   For You have delivered ***Paul's*** soul from death,
　　And prevented ***his*** feet from falling,
　　That ***Paul*** may walk before God in the light of the living.

Psalm 91:5-7   ***Paul*** shall not be afraid of the terror by night,
　　Nor of the arrow that flies by day;
　　Nor of the pestilence that walks in darkness,
　　Nor of the destruction that lays waste at noonday. A thousand may
　　　　fall at ***Paul's*** side,
　　And ten thousand at ***his*** right hand;
　　But it will not come near ***him***.

Psalm 97:10   ***Paul*** loves the LORD and hates evil.
　　He preserves ***Paul's*** soul, because ***Paul*** is one of His saints.
　　He delivers ***Paul*** out of the hand of the wicked.

Psalm 121:5-7   The LORD is ***Paul's*** keeper.
　　The LORD is ***his*** shade on ***his*** right hand.
The sun will not harm ***Paul*** by day,
　　Nor the moon by night.
Peace be within your walls,
　　And prosperity within your palaces.

Psalm 146:8   The LORD opens ***Paul's*** eyes when ***he*** is blind.
　　The LORD raises up ***Paul*** when ***he*** is bowed down.
　　The LORD loves ***Paul*** because ***he*** is righteous.

Psalm 147:3   He heals ***Paul's*** broken heart,
　　And binds up ***his*** wounds.

　　Isaiah 19:22   Yahweh will strike Egypt, striking and healing. They will return to Yahweh, and He will be entreated by them, and will heal them.

　　Isaiah 29:18   In that day, the deaf will hear the words of the book, and the eyes of the blind will see out of obscurity and out of darkness.
Isaiah 35:4-6   Tell those who have a fearful heart, "Be strong. Don't be afraid. Behold, your God will come with vengeance, God's retribution. He will come and save you. Then the eyes of the blind will be opened,

and the ears of the deaf will be unstopped. Then the lame man will leap like a deer, and the tongue of the mute will sing; for waters will break out in the wilderness, and streams in the desert.

Isaiah 38:15-16   What will I say? He has both spoken to me, and Himself has done it. I will walk carefully all my years because of the anguish of my soul. Lord, men live by these things; and my spirit finds life in all of them: You restore me, and cause me to live.

Isaiah 43:2   When *Paul* passes through the waters, I will be with *him*; and through the rivers, they will not overflow *him*. When *Paul* walks through the fire, *he* will not be burned, and flame will not scorch *him*.

Isaiah 53:4-5   Surely He has borne *Paul's* sickness, and carried *Paul's* suffering; yet *Paul* considered Him plagued, struck by God, and afflicted. But He was pierced for *Paul's* transgressions. He was crushed for *Paul's* iniquities. The punishment that brought *his* peace was on Him; and by His wounds *Paul* is healed.

Isaiah 54:17   "No weapon that is formed against *Paul* will prevail; and *he* will condemn every tongue that rises against *him* in judgment. This is *Paul's* heritage as a servant of Yahweh, and *his* righteousness which is of Me," says Yahweh.

Isaiah 58:6-11   Isn't this the fast that I have chosen: that *Paul* loose the bonds of wickedness, that *he* undo the bands of the yoke, and let the oppressed go free, and that *Paul* break every yoke? Isn't it to distribute *his* bread to the hungry, and that *Paul* bring the poor who are cast out to *his* house? When *Paul* sees the naked, that *he* cover *him*; and that *Paul* not hide *himself* from *his* own flesh? Then *Paul's* light shall break forth as the morning, and *his* healing shall spring forth speedily; and *Paul's* righteousness shall go before *him*; the glory of Yahweh shall be *Paul's* rear guard. Then *Paul* shall call, and Yahweh will answer; *he* shall cry, and He will say, 'Here I am.' If *Paul* takes away from *himself* the yoke, the putting forth of the finger, and speaking wickedly; and if *Paul* draws out *his* soul to the hungry, and satisfies the afflicted soul: then *Paul's* light shall rise in darkness, and *his* obscurity will be as the noonday; and

Yahweh will guide **Paul** continually, and satisfy **his** soul in dry places, and make strong **his** bones; and **Paul** shall be like a watered garden, and like a spring of water, whose waters don't fail.

Matthew 8:5-13   When Jesus came into Capernaum, a centurion came to Him, asking Him, and saying, "Lord, my servant lies in the house paralyzed, grievously tormented." Jesus said to him, *"I will come and heal him."* The centurion answered, "Lord, I'm not worthy for You to come under my roof. Just say the word, and my servant will be healed. For I am also a man under authority, having soldiers under me. I tell this one, 'Go,' and he goes; and to another, 'Come,' and he comes; and to my servant, 'Do this,' and he does it." When Jesus heard it, He marveled, and said to those who followed, *"Most assuredly I tell you, I haven't found so great a faith, not even in Israel. I tell you that many will come from the east and the west, and will sit down with Abraham, Isaac, and Jacob in the kingdom of heaven, but the sons of the kingdom will be thrown out into the outer darkness. There will be weeping and the gnashing of teeth."* Jesus said to the centurion, *"Go your way. Let it be done for you as you have believed."* His servant was healed in that hour. (Luke 7:1-10)

Matthew 9:27-30   As Jesus passed by from there, two blind men followed Him, calling out and saying, "Have mercy on us, Son of David!" When He had come into the house, the blind men came to Him. Jesus said to them, *"Do you believe that I am able to do this?"* They told Him, "Yes, Lord." Then He touched their eyes, saying, *"According to your faith be it done to you."* Their eyes were opened. Jesus strictly charged them, saying, *"See that no one knows about this."*

Matthew 10:1   He called to Himself His twelve disciples, and gave them authority over unclean spirits, to cast them out, and to heal every disease and every sickness.

Matthew 10:7-8   As **Paul** goes, **he** is to preach, saying, 'The kingdom of heaven is at hand!' **Paul** is to heal the sick, cleanse the lepers, and cast out demons. Freely **Paul** received, so freely **he** is to give.

Mark 5:35-42   While He was still speaking, they came from the synagogue ruler's house saying, "Your daughter is dead. Why bother the Teacher any more?"

But Jesus, when He heard the message spoken, immediately said to the ruler of the synagogue, *"Don't be afraid, only believe."* He allowed no one to follow Him, except Peter, James, and John the brother of James. He came to the synagogue ruler's house, and He saw an uproar, weeping, and great wailing. When He had entered in, He said to them, *"Why do you make an uproar and weep? The child is not dead, but is asleep."*

They ridiculed Him. But He, having put them all out, took the father of the child and her mother and those who were with Him, and went in where the child was lying. Taking the child by the hand, He said to her, *"Talitha cumi;"* which means, being interpreted, *"Girl, I tell you, get up."* Immediately the girl rose up, and walked, for she was twelve years old. They were overcome with great amazement.

Mark 6:13   They cast out many demons, and anointed many with oil who were sick, and healed them.

Luke 1:37   For everything spoken by God is possible.

Luke 5:15   But the report concerning Him spread much more, and great multitudes came together to hear, and to be healed by Him of their infirmities. (John 6:2)

John 1:12-13   But **Paul** received Him, and to **Paul** He gave the right to become God's **son**, because **Paul** believes in His name: who was born not of blood, nor of the will of the flesh, nor of the will of man, but of God.

John 4:46-53   Jesus came therefore again to Cana of Galilee, where He made the water into wine. There was a certain nobleman whose son was sick at Capernaum. When he heard that Jesus had come out of Judea into Galilee, he went to Him, and begged Him that He would come down and heal his son, for he was at the point of death. Jesus therefore said to him, *"Unless you see signs and wonders, you will in no way believe."*

John 6:63   *It is the Spirit who gives life. The flesh profits nothing. The words that I speak to you are spirit, and are life.*

John 8:36   *If therefore the Son makes **Paul** free, **he** will be free indeed.*

John 17:15   *I pray not that You would take **Paul** from the world, but that You would keep **him** from the evil one.*

Acts 3:1-8   Peter and John were going up into the temple at the hour of prayer, 3:00 PM. A certain man who was lame from his mother's womb was being carried, whom they laid daily at the door of the temple which is called Beautiful, to ask alms of those who entered into the temple. Seeing Peter and John about to go into the temple, he asked to receive gifts for the needy. Peter, fastening his eyes on him, as did John, said, "Look at us." He listened to them, expecting to receive something from them. But Peter said, "Silver and gold have I none, but what I have, that I give you. In the name of Jesus Christ of Nazareth, get up and walk!" He took him by the right hand, and raised him up. Immediately his feet and his ankle bones received strength. Leaping up, he stood, and began to walk. He entered with them into the temple, walking, leaping, and praising God.

Acts 5:14-15   More believers were added to the Lord, multitudes of both men and women. They even carried out the sick into the streets, and laid them on cots and mattresses, so that as Peter came by, at the least his shadow might overshadow some of them.

Acts 14:8-10   At Lystra a certain man sat, crippled in his feet, lame from his mother's womb, who had never walked. He was listening to Paul speaking, who, fastening eyes on him, and seeing that he had faith to be made whole, said with a loud voice, "Stand upright on your feet!" He leaped up and walked.

Romans 5:10   For if, while **Paul** was an enemy, **he** was reconciled to God through the death of His Son, much more, being reconciled, **Paul** will be saved by His life.

Romans 6:14   For sin will not have dominion over **Paul**. For **he** is not under law, but under grace.

Romans 8:1   There is therefore now no condemnation for **Paul** because **he** is in Christ Jesus, because **Paul** doesn't walk according to the flesh, but according to the Spirit.

Romans 8:11   But if the Spirit of Him who raised Jesus from the dead dwells in **Paul**, He who raised Christ Jesus from the dead will also give life to **his** mortal body through His Spirit who dwells in **Paul**.

Romans 8:23-33   Not only creation, but also **Paul**, because **he** has the first fruits of the Spirit, groans within **himself**, waiting for adoption, the redemption of **Paul**'s body. For **Paul** was saved in hope, but hope that is seen is not hope. For does **Paul** hope for that which **he** sees? But if **Paul** hopes for that which **he** doesn't see, **Paul** waits for it with patience. In the same way, the Spirit also helps **Paul's** weaknesses, for **Paul** doesn't know how to pray as **he** ought. But the Spirit Himself makes intercession for **Paul** with groanings which can't be uttered. He who searches the hearts knows the Spirit's mind, because He makes intercession for **Paul** according to God. We know that all things work together for **Paul's** good, because **he** loves God and is called according to His purpose. For since He foreknew **Paul**, He also predestined **him** to be conformed to the image of His Son, that He might be the firstborn among many brothers and sisters. Since He predestined **Paul**, He also called **him**. Since He called **Paul**, He also justified **him**. Since He justified **Paul**, He also glorified **him**. What then shall we say about these things? If God is for **Paul**, who can be against **him**? He who didn't spare His own Son, but delivered Him up for **Paul**, how would He not also with Him freely give **Paul** all things? Who could bring a charge against **Paul**, because **he** is one of God's elect? It is God who justifies **Paul**.

Romans 8:37   No, in all these things, **Paul** is more than a conqueror through Him who loved **him**.

Romans 10:17   So **Paul's** faith comes by hearing, and hearing by the word of God.

2 Corinthians 5:21   For Him who knew no sin He made to be sin on *Paul's* behalf; so that in Him *Paul* might become the righteousness of God.

2 Corinthians 6:2   for He says, "At an acceptable time I listened to *Paul*, In a day of salvation I helped *Paul*." Behold, now is the acceptable time. Behold, now is the day of salvation.

Galatians 3:5-7   He that supplies the Spirit to *Paul,* and works miracles for *Paul*, does He do it by the works of the law, or by hearing of faith? Even as Abraham "believed God, and it was counted to him for righteousness." Know therefore that *Paul*, because *he* is of faith, is a *son* of Abraham.

Galatians 3:13   Christ redeemed *Paul* from the curse of the law, having become a curse for *him*. For it is written, "Cursed is everyone who hangs on a tree

Galatians 3:29   If *Paul* is Christ's, then *he* is Abraham's seed and heir according to the promise.

Ephesians 1:19-21   And what is the exceeding greatness of His power toward *Paul* because *he* believes, according to the working of the strength of His might which He worked in Christ, when He raised Him from the dead, and made Him to sit at His right hand in the heavenly places, far above all rule, and authority, and power, and dominion, and every name that is named, not only in this world, but also in that which is to come.

Ephesians 3:20   Now to Him who is able to do exceedingly abundantly above all that *Paul* can ask or think, according to the power that works in *Paul.*

Ephesians 5:30   Because we are members of His body, of His flesh and bones.

Colossians 2:10   In Him *Paul* is made complete, who is the head of all principality and power.

1 Thessalonians 3:13   To the end He may establish ***Paul's*** heart blameless in holiness before ***his*** God and Father, at the coming of ***his*** Lord Jesus with ***Paul*** and all His saints.

1 Peter 2:24   He bore ***Paul's*** sins in His body on the tree, that ***Paul***, having died to sins, might live to righteousness; by His stripes ***Paul*** was healed.

2 Peter 1:3   seeing that His divine power has granted to ***Paul*** all things that pertain to life and godliness, through the knowledge of Him who called ***Paul*** by His own glory and virtue.

Chapter F

Paul's **Confession**

Psalm 19:14   Let the words of ***Paul's*** mouth and the meditation of ***his*** heart
    Be acceptable in Your sight,
    O LORD, ***Paul's*** rock, and ***his*** Redeemer.

Psalm 23:4   Even though ***Paul*** walks through the valley of the shadow of death,
    Paul will fear no evil, for You are with ***him***.
    Your rod and Your staff, they comfort ***him***.

Proverbs 6:2   ***Paul*** is trapped by the words of ***his*** mouth.
    Paul is ensnared with the words of ***his*** mouth.

Proverbs 16:24   Pleasant words are a honeycomb,
    Sweet to ***Paul's*** soul, and health to ***his*** bones.

Matthew 4:4   But He answered, *"It is written, 'Man shall not live by bread alone, but by every word that proceeds out of the mouth of God.'"*

Matthew 4:7   Jesus said to him, *"Again, it is written, 'You shall not test the Lord, your God.'"*

Matthew 4:10-11   Then Jesus said to him, *"Get behind me, Satan! For it is written, 'You shall worship the Lord your God, and Him only shall you serve.'"* Then the devil left Him, and behold, angels came and ministered to Him.

Matthew 18:19-20   *Again, assuredly I tell you, that if **Paul** and one other will agree on earth concerning anything that they will ask, it will be done for them by My Father who is in heaven. For where **Paul** and one or two others are gathered together in My name, there I am in the midst of them."* (Mk 9:33-50; Lk 9:46-62)

Matthew 24:35   *Heaven and earth will pass away, but My words will not pass away.* (Mk 13:1-37; Lk 21:5-36)

Mark 10:46-52   They came to Jericho. As He went out from Jericho, with His disciples and a great multitude, the son of Timaeus, Bartimaeus, a blind beggar, was sitting by the road. When he heard that it was Jesus the Nazarene, he began to cry out, and say, "Jesus, Son of David, have mercy on me!" Many rebuked him, that he should be quiet, but he cried out much more, "Son of David, have mercy on me!" Jesus stood still, and said, *"Call him."* They called the blind man, saying to him, "Cheer up! Get up. He is calling you!" He, casting away his cloak, sprang up, and came to Jesus. Jesus asked him, *"What do you want Me to do for you?"* The blind man said to Him, "Lord, that I may see again." Jesus said to him, *"Go your way. Your faith has made you well."* Immediately he received his sight, and followed Jesus on the road. (Lk 18:35-43)

    Mark 11:23-24   *For most assuredly I tell you, if **Paul** tells this mountain, 'Be taken up and cast into the sea,' and doesn't doubt in **his** heart, but believes that what **he** says is happening; **Paul** shall have whatever **he** says. Therefore I tell you, all things whatever **Paul** prays and asks for, if **he** believes that **he** receives them, then **he** shall have them.* (Matt 21:20-22)
Luke 18:35-43   It happened, as He came near Jericho, a blind man sat by the road, begging. Hearing a multitude going by, he asked what this

meant. They told him that Jesus of Nazareth was passing by. He cried out, "Jesus, Son of David, have mercy on me!" Those who led the way rebuked him, that he should be quiet; but he cried out all the more, "Son of David, have mercy on me!" Standing still, Jesus commanded him to be brought to Him. When he had come near, He asked him, *"What do you want Me to do?"* He said, "Lord, that I may see again." Jesus said to him, *"Receive your sight. Your faith has healed you."* Immediately he received his sight, and followed Him, glorifying God. All the people, when they saw it, praised God. (Mk 10:46-52)

John 14:13-14   Whatever **Paul** will ask in My name, that I will do, that the Father may be glorified in the Son. If **Paul** will ask anything in My name, I will do it.
John 15:7-8   If **Paul** remains in Me, and My words remain in **him**, **Paul** will ask whatever **he** desires, and it will be done for **him**.

"In this is My Father glorified, that **Paul** bears much fruit; and so **Paul** will be My disciple.

John 16:23-24   "In that day **Paul** will ask Me no questions. Most assuredly I tell you, whatever **Paul** may ask of the Father in My name, He will give it to **Paul**. Until now, **Paul** has asked nothing in My name. If **Paul** asks, **he** will receive, that **his** joy may be made full.
Acts 9:33-35   There he found a certain man named Aeneas, who had been bedridden for eight years, because he was paralyzed. Peter said to him, "Aeneas, Jesus Christ heals you. Get up and make your bed!" Immediately he arose. All who lived at Lydda and in Sharon saw him, and they turned to the Lord.

Romans 10:9-10   that if **Paul** will confess with **his** mouth the Lord Jesus, and believe in **his** heart that God raised Him from the dead, **Paul** will be saved. For with the heart, **Paul** believes unto righteousness; and with the mouth confession is made unto salvation. For the Scripture says, "If **Paul** believes in Him, **he** will not be put to shame."

Philippians 2:8-11   And being found in human form, He humbled Himself, becoming obedient to death, yes, the death of the cross. Therefore God also highly exalted Him, and gave Him the name which is above every name; that at the name of Jesus every knee should bow, of those in heaven, those on earth, and those under the earth, and that every tongue should confess that Jesus Christ is Lord, to the glory of God the Father.

Hebrews 4:14-16   Having then a great High Priest, who has passed through the heavens, Jesus, the Son of God, let **Paul** hold tightly to **his** confession. For **Paul** doesn't have a High Priest who can't be touched with the feelings of **Paul's** infirmities, but He has been in all points tempted like **Paul** is, yet without sin. Let **Paul** therefore draw near with boldness to the throne of grace, that **he** may receive mercy, and may find grace in time of need.

Hebrews 10:23   Let **Paul** hold fast the confession of **his** hope without wavering. For He who promised is faithful.

James 5:15-16   And the prayer of faith will heal **Paul** when **he** is sick, and the Lord will raise **him** up. If **Paul** has committed sins, **he** will be forgiven. If **Paul** confesses **his** offenses to others, and prays with others, then **Paul** will be healed. The earnest prayer of a righteous **man** like **Paul** is powerful and effective.

1 John 5:14-15   This is the boldness which **Paul** has toward Him, that, if **Paul** asks anything according to His will, He listens to **him**. And if **Paul** knows that He listens to **him**, whatever **Paul** asks, **he** knows that **he** has the petitions which **he** has asked of Him.

Chapter G

Strength

Exodus 15:2   Yah is **Paul's** strength and song. He has become **Paul's** salvation. This is **his** God, and **Paul** will praise Him; **his** father's God, and **Paul** will exalt Him.

Deuteronomy 34:7   Moses was one hundred twenty years old when he died: his eye was not dim, nor his natural force abated.

2 Samuel 22:3-4   God, **Paul's** rock, in Him **he** will take refuge; **Paul's** shield, and the horn of **his** salvation, **Paul's** high tower, and **his** refuge. **Paul's** savior, You save **him** from violence. **Paul** will call on Yahweh, who is worthy to be praised: So shall **Paul** be saved from **his** enemies.

2 Samuel 22:33-34   God is **Paul's** strong fortress. He makes **Paul's** way perfect. He makes **his** feet like hinds' feet, and sets **Paul** on **his** high places.

1 Chronicles 16:11-12   Seek Yahweh, **Paul**, and His strength. Seek His face forever more. Remember His marvelous works, **Paul**, that He has done, His wonders, and the judgments of His mouth,

2 Chronicles 16:9a   For the eyes of Yahweh run back and forth throughout the whole earth, to show Himself strong in the behalf of **Paul** because **his** heart is perfect toward Him.

Nehemiah 8:10   Then he said to them, "Go your way. Eat the fat, drink the sweet, and send portions to him for whom nothing is prepared; for this day is holy to **Paul's** Lord. Don't be grieved, **Paul**, for the joy of Yahweh is your strength."

Job 5:26   **Paul** shall come to **his** grave in a full age, like a shock of grain comes in its season.

Job 17:9   Yet shall the righteous hold on his way. He who has clean hands shall grow stronger and stronger.

Psalm 18:1-3   **Paul** loves You, O LORD, **his** strength.
The LORD is **Paul's** rock, **his** fortress, and **his** deliverer;
　　Paul's God, **his** rock, in whom **he** takes refuge;
　　Paul's shield, and the horn of **his** salvation, **his** high tower.
Paul calls on the LORD, who is worthy to be praised;
　　And **he** is saved from **his** enemies.

Psalm 18:32   The God who arms **Paul** with strength, and makes **his** way perfect?

Psalm 19:14   Let the words of **Paul's** mouth and the meditation of **his** heart
　　Be acceptable in Your sight,

O LORD, ***Paul's*** rock, and ***his*** Redeemer.

Psalm 29:11   The LORD will give strength to ***Paul***.
   The LORD will bless ***Paul*** with peace.

Psalm 34:19-20   Many are ***Paul's*** afflictions,
   but the LORD delivers ***Paul*** out of them all.
He protects all of ***his*** bones.
   Not one of them is broken.

Psalm 41:3   The LORD will sustain ***Paul*** on ***his*** sickbed,
   And restore ***Paul*** from ***his*** bed of illness.

Psalm 46:1-3   God is ***Paul's*** refuge and strength,
   A very present help in trouble.
Therefore ***Paul*** won't be afraid, though the earth changes,
   Though the mountains are shaken into the heart of the seas;
   Though the waters of it roar and are troubled,
   Though the mountains tremble.
Selah.

Psalm 68:35   You are awesome, O God, in Your sanctuaries.
   The God of Israel gives strength and power to ***Paul***.
   Praise be to God!

Psalm 73:26   ***Paul's*** flesh and ***his*** heart fail,
   But God is the strength of ***Paul's*** heart and ***his*** portion forever.

Psalm 77:14-15   You are the God who does wonders.
   You have made Your strength known among the peoples.
You have redeemed Your people with Your arm,
   The sons of Jacob and Joseph.
Selah.

Psalm 103:2-5   Praise the LORD, ***Paul's*** soul,
   And don't forget all His benefits;
Who forgives all of ***Paul's*** sins;
   Who heals all of ***Paul's*** diseases;
Who redeems ***Paul's*** life from destruction;
   Who crowns ***Paul*** with steadfast love and tender mercies;
Who satisfies ***Paul's*** desire with good things,

So that ***Paul's*** youth is renewed like the eagle's.

Psalm 103:20   Praise the L ORD, you His angels,
   Who are mighty in strength, who fulfill His word,
   Obeying the voice of His word.

Psalm 105:4-5   Seek the L ORD and His strength, ***Paul***.
   Seek His face forever more.
Remember His marvelous works that He has done, ***Paul***;
   His wonders, and the judgments of His mouth.

Psalm 118:14   The L ORD is ***Paul's*** strength and song.
   He has become ***Paul's*** salvation.

Psalm 119:50   This is ***Paul's*** comfort in ***his*** affliction,
   For Your word has revived ***him***.

Proverbs 3:7-8   ***Paul*** must not be wise in ***his*** own eyes.
   Paul is to fear the L ORD, and depart from evil.
For it will be health to ***Paul's*** body,
   And nourishment to ***his*** bones.

   Isaiah 12:2-5   Behold, God is ***Paul's*** salvation. ***Paul*** will trust, and will not be afraid; for Yahweh, is ***Paul's*** strength and song; and He has become ***his*** salvation." Therefore with joy ***Paul*** will draw water out of the wells of salvation. In that day ***Paul*** will say, "Give thanks to Yahweh! Call on His name, ***Paul***. Declare His doings among the peoples. Proclaim that His name is exalted! Sing to Yahweh, ***Paul***, for He has done excellent things! Let this be known in all the earth!"
Isaiah 40:29-31   He gives power to the weak. He increases ***Paul's*** strength when ***he*** has no might. Even the youths faint and get weary, and the young men utterly fall; But if ***Paul*** waits for Yahweh He will renew ***his*** strength. ***Paul*** will mount up with wings like eagles; ***he*** will run, and not be weary, ***he*** will walk, and not faint.

   Isaiah 41:10   ***Paul*** should not be afraid, for I am with ***him***.   ***Paul*** should not be dismayed, for I am ***his*** God. I will strengthen ***Paul***. Yes, I will help ***him***. Yes, I will uphold ***Paul*** with the right hand of My righteousness.

   Jeremiah 16:19   Yahweh, ***Paul's*** strength, and ***his*** stronghold, and

Paul's refuge in the day of affliction, to You shall the nations come from the ends of the earth, and shall say, "Our fathers have inherited nothing but lies, even vanity and things in which there is no profit."

Ezekiel 34:16   I will seek that which was lost, and will bring back that which was driven away, and will bind up that which was broken, and will strengthen that which was sick: but the fat and the strong I will destroy; I will feed them in justice.
Joel 3:10   ***Paul*** shall beat ***his*** plowshare into a sword, and ***his*** pruning hooks into spears. Let ***Paul***, when ***he*** is weak, say, 'I am strong.'

Habakkuk 3:19   Yahweh, the Lord, is ***Paul's*** strength. He makes ***Paul's*** feet like deer's feet, and enables ***Paul*** to go in high places.

Malachi 4:2   But to ***Paul*** who fears My name shall the sun of righteousness arise with healing in its wings. ***Paul*** will go out, and leap like a calf of the stall.

Acts 3:7   He took him by the right hand, and raised him up. Immediately his feet and his ankle bones received strength.

Acts 14:8-10   At Lystra a certain man sat, crippled in his feet, lame from his mother's womb, who had never walked. He was listening to Paul speaking, who, fastening eyes on him, and seeing that he had faith to be made whole, said with a loud voice, "Stand upright on your feet!" He leaped up and walked.

Romans 5:6-8   For while ***Paul*** was yet weak, at the right time Christ died for ***him***. For one will hardly die for a righteous person. Yet perhaps for a good person someone would dare to die. But God shows His love toward ***Paul***, in that while ***Paul*** was yet a sinner, Christ died for ***him***.

2 Corinthians 12:9-10   He said to me, "My grace is sufficient for ***Paul***, for My power is made perfect in ***Paul's*** weakness." Most gladly therefore ***Paul*** will rather glory in ***his*** weaknesses, that the power of Christ may rest on ***Paul***. Therefore I take pleasure in weaknesses, in injuries, in necessities, in persecutions, in distresses, for Christ's sake. For when ***Paul*** is weak, then ***he*** is strong.

Philippians 4:13   ***Paul*** can do all things through Christ, who strengthens *him*.

1 Timothy 1:12   *Paul* thanks Him who enabled *him*, Christ Jesus, *his* Lord, because He counted *Paul* faithful, appointing *him* to service;

Hebrews 11:11   By faith, even Sarah herself received power to conceive, and she bore a child when she was past age, since she counted Him faithful who had promised.

1 Peter 5:10   But may the God of all grace (who called *Paul* to His eternal glory by Christ Jesus), after *Paul* has suffered a while, perfect, establish, strengthen, and settle *Paul*.

Chapter H

Paul **Must Choose Life**

Deuteronomy 30:19-20   I call heaven and earth to witness against *Paul* this day, that I have set before *him* life and death, the blessing and the curse: therefore *Paul* should choose life, that *he* may live, *Paul* and *his* seed; *Paul* is to love Yahweh *his* God, to obey His voice, and to cleave to Him; for He is *Paul's* life, and the length of *his* days; that *Paul* `may dwell in the land which Yahweh swore to *his* fathers, to Abraham, to Isaac, and to Jacob, to give them.

Psalm 118:17   *Paul* will not die, but live, And declare the works of the LORD.

Proverbs 15:30   A cheerful look brings *Paul's* heart joy. Good news gives health to *his* bones.

Luke 8:43-48   A woman who had a flow of blood for twelve years, who had spent all her living on physicians, and could not be healed by any, came behind Him, and touched the fringe of His cloak, and immediately the flow of her blood stopped. Jesus said, *"Who touched Me?"* When all denied it, Peter and those with Him said, "Master, the multitudes press and jostle You, and You say, 'Who touched Me?' "But Jesus said, *"Someone did touch Me, for I perceived that power has gone out of Me."* When the woman saw that she was not hidden, she came trembling, and falling down before Him declared to Him in the presence of all the people the reason why she had touched Him, and how she was healed immediately. He said to her, *"Daughter, cheer up. Your faith has made you well. Go in peace."* (Matt 9:20-22; Mk 5:25-34)

Luke 8:49-55   While He still spoke, one from the ruler of the synagogue's house came, saying to him, "Your daughter is dead. Don't trouble the Teacher." But Jesus hearing it, answered him, *"Don't be afraid. Only believe, and she will be healed."* When He came to the house, He didn't allow anyone to enter in, except Peter, John, James, the father of the child, and her mother. All were weeping and mourning, but He said, *"Don't weep. She isn't dead, but sleeping."*

They were ridiculing Him, knowing that she was dead. But He put them all outside, and taking her by the hand, He called, saying, *"Child, arise!"* Her spirit returned, and she rose up immediately. He commanded that something be given to her to eat. (Matt. 9:23-26; Mk 5:24, 35-43)

Luke 9:38-42   Behold, a man from the crowd called out, saying, "Teacher, I beg You to look at my son, for he is my only child. Behold, a spirit takes him, he suddenly cries out, and it convulses him so that he foams, and it hardly ever leaves him, bruising him severely. I begged Your disciples to cast it out, and they couldn't."Jesus answered, *"Faithless and perverse generation, how long shall I be with you and bear with you? Bring your son here."*

While he was still coming, the demon threw him down and convulsed him violently. But Jesus rebuked the unclean spirit, and healed the boy, and gave him back to his father.   (Matt 17:14-21; Mk 9:14-29)

Luke 14:24   *For I tell you that none of those men who were invited will taste of my supper.'"*

John 11:21-27   Martha said to Jesus, "Lord, if You would have been here, my brother wouldn't have died. Even now I know that, whatever You ask of God, God will give You." Jesus said to her, *"Your brother will rise again."* Martha said to Him, "I know that he will rise again in the resurrection at the last day." Jesus said to her, *"I am the resurrection* and the life. If **Paul** believes in Me, though **he** die, yet will **he** live. If **Paul** lives and believes in Me, **he** will never die. Do you believe this?" She said to Him, "Yes, Lord. I have come to believe that You are the Christ, God's Son, He who comes into the world."

John 11:39-44   Jesus said, *"Take away the stone."* Martha, the sister of him who was dead, said to Him, "Lord, by this time there is a stench, for he has been dead four days." Jesus said to her, *"Didn't I tell you that if you believed, you would see God's glory?"* So they took away the stone from the place where the dead man was lying. Jesus lifted up His eyes, and said, *"Father, I thank You that You listened to Me. I know that You always listen to Me, but because of the multitude that stands around I said this, that they may believe that You sent Me."* When He had said this, He cried with a loud voice, *"Lazarus, come out!"* He who was dead came out, bound hand and foot with wrappings, and his face was wrapped around with a cloth. Jesus said to them, *"Free him, and let him go."*

GOD'S HEALING POWER THROUGH YOU

Teaching/Study Outline

By Paul and Lynn Crawford

SESSION ONE

Jesus' Vision for the Believer were his last recorded words

> Mark 16:17-18   These miraculous signs will accompany those who believe: They will cast out demons in my name, and they will speak in new languages.
> 18 They will be able to handle snakes with safety,

and if they drink anything poisonous, it won't hurt them. They will be able to place their hands on the sick, and they will be healed. NLT

The translation below adds "believers who believe"

Mark 16:17-19   And signs shall accompany those believing these things; in my name demons they shall cast out; with new tongues they shall speak; 18 serpents they shall take up; and if any deadly thing they may drink, it shall not hurt them; on the ailing they shall lay hands, and they shall be well. 19 The Lord, then, indeed, after speaking to them, was received up to the heaven, and sat on the right hand of God; YLT Young's Literal Translation

Jesus' Vision is Worldwide: Beginning with the disciples, believers have been fulfilling this commandment

Charles and Frances Hunter's Vision
1. Worldwide Lay Evangelists and authors of 93 books.
2. Committed to God's Word and His Kingdom.
3. Since becoming Spirit filled, focus has been ministry, healing and evangelism.
4. Saw the need to train others to reach the sick.
5. Believe the supernatural power of God can be taught.
6. Given vision of Houston Astrodome "Healing Explosion."
7. First Explosion held July 4, 1985 in Pittsburgh.
8. Astrodome Healing Explosion

It is God's Will and Nature That You Be Healed

3 John 2:2   Beloved, I pray that you may prosper in all things and be in health, just as your soul prospers. NKJV

Jehovah Rophe: I am the God who heals

26 He said, If you will listen carefully to the voice of the Lord your God and do what is right in his sight, obeying his commands and keeping all his decrees, then I will not make you suffer any of the diseases I sent on the Egyptians; for I am the Lord who heals you. NLT

One third of Jesus' recorded ministry was Healing

I come to do the work of the Father…

John 5:30:30   I can do nothing on my own. I judge as God tells me. Therefore, my judgment is just, because I carry out the will of the one who sent me, not my own will. NLT

Jesus bore our Infirmities

Matt 8:16   That evening many demon-possessed people were brought to Jesus. He cast out the evil spirits with a simple command, and he healed all the sick. 17 This fulfilled the word of the Lord through the prophet Isaiah, who said, He took our sicknesses and removed our diseases.   NLT

God is no respecter of persons

Acts 10:34   And Peter opened his mouth and said: Most certainly and thoroughly I now perceive and understand that God shows no partiality and is no respecter of persons, AMP

God's Provision For Healing

Jesus came to destroy the works of the devil

1 John 3:8:8   But when people keep on sinning, it shows that they belong to the devil, who has been sinning since the beginning. But the Son of God came to destroy the works of the devil. NLT

Jesus personally paid the painful price for our healing

1 Peter 2:24:24   He personally carried our sins in his body on the cross so that we can be dead to sin and live for what is right. By his wounds you are healed. NLT

Jesus paid the price on the cross... PAID IN FULL.

Jesus Told Us To Heal The Sick

Matt 10:8   Heal the sick, raise the dead, cure those with leprosy, and cast out demons. Give as freely as you have received! NLT

Don't "pass the buck". Jesus...please heal this person!

Jesus said "It is finished..." –Now it is <u>our</u> turn!

Matt 12:50   Anyone who does the will of my Father in heaven is my brother and sister and mother! NLT

Mark 16:17-18   These miraculous signs will accompany those who believe: They will cast out demons in my name, and they will speak in new languages. 18 They will be able to handle snakes with safety, and if they drink anything poisonous, it won't hurt them. They will be able to place their hands on the sick, and they will be healed. NLT

John 14:12-14   I tell you the truth, anyone who believes in me will do the same works I have done, and even greater works, because I am going to be with the Father. NLT

Preparation for ministry

Pray in the Spirit to build up your spirit

1 Cor. 14:4   A person who speaks in tongues is strengthened personally, but one who speaks a word of prophecy strengthens the entire church. NLT

1 Cor. 14:14-15   For if I pray in tongues, my spirit is praying, but I don't understand what I am saying. 15 Well then, what shall I do? I will pray in the spirit, and I will also pray in words I understand. I will sing in the spirit, and I will also sing in words I understand. NLT

Fast and pray before ministry for spiritual strength

Matt. 17:21   Howbeit this kind goeth not out but by prayer and fasting. KJV

Acts 10:30-31 And Cornelius said, Four days ago I

> *was fasting until this hour; and at the ninth hour I prayed in my house, and, behold, a man stood before me in bright clothing, 31 And said, Cornelius, thy prayer is heard, and thine alms are had in remembrance in the sight of God. KJV*

> *Acts 14:23   And when they had ordained them elders in every church, and had prayed with fasting, they commended them to the Lord, on whom they believed. KJV*

> *Luke 5:33   They said to him, "John's disciples often fast and pray" NIV*

Study God's word and Pray the Scripture, not the problem.

A Healing Model: Speaking Word of Command

I cannot find any scripture where Jesus prayed for anyone to be healed, and the Apostles never prayed for anyone to be healed after Pentecost (that is recorded in Scripture). They commanded healing and spent time in prayer, to build up their Spirit to minister and deepen their own personal relationship with the Lord. One passage is sometimes thought to be a prayer. The scriptures indicate:

> *Mark 7:32-35 A deaf man with a speech impediment was brought to him, and the people begged Jesus to lay his hands on the man to heal him. 33 Jesus led him away from the crowd so they could be alone. He put his fingers into the man's ears. Then, spitting on his own fingers, he touched the man's tongue. 34* **Looking up to heaven, he**

sighed and said, "Ephphatha," which means, "Be opened!" 35 Instantly the man could hear perfectly, and his tongue was freed so he could speak plainly! NLT

Command afflicted body parts to become healed and/or restored

"In the name of Jesus, by the power of the Holy Spirit I command you (leg, arm, eye, heart, lung, etc...) to be healed."

Luke 4:39   Standing at her bedside, he rebuked the fever, and it left her. And she got up at once and prepared a meal for them. NLT

Mark 9:25   When Jesus saw that the crowd of onlookers was growing, he rebuked the evil spirit. Listen, you spirit that makes this boy unable to hear and speak, he said. I command you to come out of this child and never enter him again! NLT

Mark 4:39   When Jesus woke up, he rebuked the wind and said to the water, "Silence! Be still!" Suddenly the wind stopped, and there was a great calm. NLT

Matt 17:18   Then Jesus rebuked the demon in the boy, and it left him. From that moment the boy was well. NLT

Jesus often required the person to take a Faith Action: <u>Mark 3:5</u>: "Stretch forth thy arm..." <u>John 9:6-8</u>: "Go and wash in the pool...", or as Elisha commanded Naaman in <u>2 Kings 5:14</u>: "...dip in the river seven times...".

Mark 3:5   Then he said to the man, "Hold out your hand." So the man held out his hand, and it was restored! NLT

John 9:6-7   Then he spit on the ground, made mud with the saliva, and spread the mud over the blind man's eyes. 7 He told him, "Go wash yourself in the pool of Siloam" (Siloam means "sent"). So the man went and washed and came back seeing! NLT

2 Kings 5:10   But Elisha sent a messenger out to him with this message: "Go and wash yourself seven times in the Jordan River. Then your skin will be restored, and you will be healed of your leprosy." NLT

2 Kings 5:13-14   But his officers tried to reason with him and said, "Sir, if the prophet had told you to do something very difficult, wouldn't you have done it? So you should certainly obey him when he says simply, 'Go and wash and be cured!'" 14 So Naaman went down to the Jordan River and dipped himself seven times, as the man of God had instructed him. And his skin became as healthy as the skin of a young child's, and he was healed! NLT

SESSION TWO

1. ***Know Jesus as your personal Savior and Lord***
   - a) ***Be in open communication with Him***
   - b) ***Be tuned into the Holy Spirit***
   - c) ***It's easy to minister Salvation....***

Jesus is the only way *Acts 4:10-12   Let me clearly state to all of you and to all the people of Israel that he was healed by the powerful name of Jesus Christ the Nazarene, the man you crucified but whom God raised from the dead. 11 For Jesus is the one referred to in the Scriptures, where it says, 'The stone that you builders rejected has now become the cornerstone.' 12 There is salvation in no one else! God has given no other name under heaven by which we must be saved. NLT*

We all need a Savior *Heb 10:12-14 But our High Priest offered himself to God as a single sacrifice for sins, good for all time. Then he sat down in the place of honor at God's right hand. 13 There he waits until his enemies are humbled and made a footstool under his feet. 14 For by that one offering he forever made perfect those who are being made holy. NLT*

God loves us *John 3:16-17   For God loved the world so much that he gave his one and only Son, so* that everyone who believes in him will not perish but have eternal life. 17 God sent his Son into the world not to judge the world, but to save the world through him.

Jesus paid it all 1 John 1:7   But if we are living in the light, as God is in the light, then we have fellowship with each other, and the blood of Jesus, his Son, cleanses us from all sin.

Believe and confess Rom 10:9   If you confess with your mouth that Jesus is Lord and believe in your heart that God raised him from the dead, you will be saved. 10 For it is by believing in your heart that you are made right with God, and it is by confessing with your mouth that you are saved. 11 As the Scriptures tell us, 'Anyone who trusts in him will never be disgraced.'

Salvation is assured John 5:24   I tell you the truth, those who listen to my message and believe in God who sent me have eternal life. They will never be condemned for their sins, but they have already passed from death into life. NLT

Sample Prayer

"Lord, I have sinned, forgive me all my sins. I believe You died for me and rose again that I might have new life In You. I know You are the only begotten Son of the Father. Please come Into my life. Help me to follow You and obey and make me what You created me to be. I invite you to be Lord of my life. I believe you have cleansed me with your blood and forgiven me all my sins. Thank you for redeeming me out of the dominion of darkness and transferring me into the kingdom of Your Glorious Light. Amen."

2. **Baptism in Holy Spirit with speaking in tongues**

   a) *1 Cor. 14:4 He who speaks in a tongue edifies himself, NKJV*

   b) *It's easy to minister the Baptism in the Holy Spirit:*

   c) *Jesus is the baptizer. He will baptize you with the Holy Spirit.*

Mark 1:7-8 John announced: Someone is coming soon who is greater than I am—so much greater that I'm not even worthy to stoop down like a slave and untie the straps of his sandals. 8 I baptize you with water, but he will baptize you with the Holy Spirit!

It is for everyone. Acts 2:38-40   Peter replied, "Each of you must repent of your sins, turn to God, and be baptized in the name of Jesus Christ to show that you have received forgiveness for your sins. Then you will receive the gift of the Holy Spirit. 39 This promise is to you, and to your children, and even to the Gentiles—all who have been called by the Lord our God."

Luke 11:13 So if you sinful people know how to give good gifts to your children, how much more will your heavenly Father give the Holy Spirit to those   who ask him.

Sample Prayer

"Jesus, I believe You are the baptizer in the Holy Spirit. Father, cleanse me from all unrighteousness and fill me NOW, with Your Holy Spirit. In faith I will receive. I will open my mouth and speak the unknown tongue I receive from you as I speak."

[Note: If a person seems blocked from receiving, there could be a need to renounce cult or occult activities that may have caused contamination by enemy spirits.]

3. **Places of Agreement**

   a) *He has no point of agreement. I am a child of God. He has nothing in common with me (sin, occult activities, and possessions). There is nothing in me that belongs to him. (attitudes, secrets).*

   b) *He has no power over me.*

   John 14:30 (Amplified)...I will not talk with you much more, for the prince (evil genius, ruler) of the world is coming. And he has no claim on Me.

   John 14:30   I don't have much more time to talk to you, because the ruler of this world approaches. He has no power over me NLT

4. **Holiness**

   a) **Establish a clear channel**

Ps. 24:3-5   Who may climb the mountain of the Lord? Who may stand in his holy place? 4 Only those whose hands and hearts are pure, who do not worship idols and never tell lies. 5 They will receive the Lord's blessing and have a right relationship with God their savior. NLT

b) Go and sin no more

Rom 6:11-13   So you also should consider yourselves to be dead to the power of sin and alive to God through Christ Jesus. 12 Do not let sin control the way you live; do not give in to sinful desires. 13 Do not let any part of your body become an instrument of evil to serve sin. Instead, give yourselves completely to God, for you were dead, but now you have new life.

c) Keep His commandments

Deut 28:1-2   If you fully obey the Lord your God and carefully keep all his commands that I am giving you today, the Lord your God will set you high above all the nations of the world. 2 You will experience all these blessings if you obey the Lord your God. NLT

5. Accursed Things

a) *Deut. 7:25,26   The graven Images of their gods you shall burn with fire; you shall not desire the silver or gold that is on them, NOR TAKE IT FOR YOURSELF, LEST YOU BE ENSNARED BY IT; for It is an abomination to the Lord your God. Neither shall you bring an abomination INTO YOUR HOUSE, LEST YOU BECOME AN ACCURSED THING LIKE IT; but you shall utterly detest and abhor It, for it is an accursed thing.*

Categories of accursed things: (incomplete listing): Buddha's, temples, tiki gods, monkey gods, occult objects, occult rock groups, some toys and games (Dungeons and Dragons, He-man, etc.), some cartoons and movies, books, jewelry (Egyptian, occult, etc.), crystals, pyramids, and art depicting occult or false religion practices.

6. Desire Spiritual Gifts

a) Expect gifts of the Spirit to flow through you as needed to do the works of Jesus and build the individual and the church body.

b) Situational gifts (and situations where someone is in need): *1 Cor. 12:7-11 A spiritual gift is given to each of us so we can help each other. 8 To one person the Spirit gives the ability to give wise advice; to another the same Spirit gives a message of special knowledge. 9 The same Spirit gives great faith to another, and to someone else the one Spirit gives the gift of healing. 10 He gives one person the power to perform miracles, and another the ability to prophesy. He gives someone else the ability to discern whether a message is from the Spirit of God or from another spirit. Still another person is given the ability to speak in unknown languages, while another is given the ability to interpret what is being said. 11 It is the one and only Spirit who distributes all these gifts. He alone decides which gift each person should have. NLT*

    c) Paul said it was good for the Body of Christ to desire Spiritual Gifts:*1 Cor. 14:14 Let love be your highest goal! But you should also desire the special abilities the Spirit gives—especially the ability to prophesy.*

    d) 2 Kings 2:9-16 Elisha asked for a double portion and got it. Be spiritually greedy!

7. *Ministering By The Power of the Holy Spirit*

    a) *Acts 10:38* Jesus didn't minister healing and miracles until the Holy Spirit came upon Him. *"...how God anointed Jesus of Nazareth with the Holy Spirit and with power, and how he went about doing good and healing all who were under the power of the Devil, because God was with him."*

    b) *John 5:3-6,8* Jesus was led by the Spirit to heal certain people. *"...there a great number of disabled people used to lie— the blind, the lame, the paralyzed. One who was there had been an Invalid for thirty eight years. When Jesus saw him lying there and learned that he had been In this condition for a long time, he asked him do you want to get well?" ... "Then Jesus said to him, 'Get up! Pick up your mat and walk.' At once the man was cured...."*

    c) *Acts 9:17* Paul ministered healing empowered by the

Spirit. *"...then Ananias went to the house and entered it. Placing his hands on Saul, he said 'Brother Saul, the Lord Jesus who appeared to you on the road as you were coming here— has sent me so that you may see again and be filled with the Holy Spirit.' Immediately something like scales fell from Saul's eyes, and he could see again."*

8. Invite the Holy Spirit to flow through you.... Word Of Knowledge

a) Seek the word from God for the need... Word, picture, memory, emotion, body sensation or pain...

b) Allow your inner sensing to be vocalized.

c) A true word will bring healing by newfound Faith.

d) Cold reading (from sight or knowledge of an individual's past) not by the Spirit

e) Call to integrity: *"I sense"* may be better than GOD TOLD ME.

f) Person receiving is the "umpire". The word will confirm or reveal the truth.

9. Line Up With Jesus

a) *John 15:5* Align with Jesus. *"I am the vine, you are the branches. If a man remains in me and I in him, he will bear much fruit; apart from me you can do nothing."*

b) *John 8:28*   Spend time listening to His voice. *"So Jesus said, 'When you have lifted up the Son of Man, then you will know who I am, and that I do nothing on my own but speak just what the Father has taught me."*

c) *John 5:19* See results in the spirit. *"...Jesus gave them this answer: 'I tell you the truth, the Son can do nothing by Himself; He can do only what He sees His Father doing, because whatever the Father does the Son also does."*

10. Healing is the Servant of Evangelism

a) Before or after healing ministry...ask them, *"do they know Jesus personally?"*

b) *Acts 5:12-14*   Healing is to Glorify the Father, not us, and to lead to Jesus. *"Nevertheless, more and more men and women believed In the Lord and were added to their number"*.

c) *Acts 9:34*   They will sometimes open in their spirit when they or someone they know is healed. *"Aeneas', Peter said to him, 'Jesus Christ heals you. Get up and take care of your mat.' Immediately Aeneas got up. All those who saw him turned to the Lord."*

d) *Heb 10:25* Get them into relationship with local church. *"..let us not give up meeting together, as some are in the habit of doing, but let us encourage one another all the more as you see the Day approaching."*

11. Initial Ministry Contact

a) Introduce yourself

b) Ask: *"What do you need?"* Listen closely on two channels; Natural and Spiritual. Either silently or aloud: *"Lord, show me the key ministry form, what You want to do."*

c) Tell them "That's easy!" Plant seed of faith in them.

d) Invite the Holy Spirit to manifest himself powerfully and expect unique gifting.

e) Do ministry Faith Form in cooperation with Holy Spirit

12. Upper Back Adjustment Model

a) Nose and toes in the same direction.

b) Lock elbows and point arms firmly straight ahead.

c) Separate palms 1/4 inch apart and support hands.

SESSION THREE

1. ***Know who you are in Jesus***

   a. *1 John 4:4 You dear children, are from God and have overcome them, because the one who is in you is greater than the one that is in the world."* The Greater One Is In you!

   b. *Luke 10:19 Jesus said I have given you authority to trample on snakes, scorpions and to overcome all the power of the enemy: Nothing will harm you.* You have the power over all the enemy's works!

   c. *Acts 1:8 But you will receive power when the Holy Spirit comes on you.*

   d. *Eph 1:18-22 "...I pray also that the eyes of your heart may be enlightened in order that you may know the hope to which he has called you, the riches of his glorious inheritance in the saints, and his incomparably great power for us who believe. That power is like the working of his mighty strength which he exerted in Christ when he raised him from the dead and seated him at his right hand in the heavenly realms, far above all rule and authority, power and dominion, and every title that can be given, not only in the present age but also in the one to come."*

   e. *Eph 3:16-17 I pray that out of his glorious riches he may strengthen you with the power through his Spirit In your Inner being so that Christ may dwell In your heart through faith."*

   f. Because of whose you are, speak with authority (it is

not necessary to be loud).

g. Command directly.

2. **Fear Of Moving Out**

   a) *2 Tim 1:7 Fear is not from God. For God did not give us a spirit of timidity, but a spirit of power, of love and of self-discipline.*

   b) *1 John 4:18   There is no fear in love. But perfect love drives out fear because fear has to do with punishment. The man who fears is not made perfect in love.*

   c) *1 Cor 13:8   God's love flowing through you will meet the need. "Love never fails."*

   d) *2 Tim. 3:17   Immerse yourself in the promises of God's Word for healing deliverance, in whatever area you lack confidence. "All scripture Is God—breathed and is useful for teaching, rebuking, correcting and training in righteousness, so that the man of God may be thoroughly equipped for every good work."*

   e) *2 Cor. 3:6 "He has made us competent as ministers of a new covenant— Not of the letter but of the Spirit; for the letter kills, but the Spirit gives life."*

3. **Miracles**

   a) Creative Miracles

   b) By Proxy

   c) **The Centurion,** *Matt. 8:8   But the officer said, "Lord, I am not worthy to have you come into my home.*

Just say the word from where you are, and my servant will be healed. 9 I know this because I am under the authority of my superior officers, and I have authority over my soldiers. I only need to say, 'Go,' and they go, or 'Come,' and they come. And if I say to my slaves, 'Do this,' they do it." 10 When Jesus heard this, he was amazed. Turning to those who were following him, he said, "I tell you the truth, I haven't seen faith like this in all Israel! NLT

d) **The Canaanite woman,** *Matt. 15:21-28   Leaving that place, Jesus withdrew to the region of Tyre and Sidon. 22 A Canaanite woman from that vicinity came to him, crying out, "Lord, Son of David, have mercy on me! My daughter is suffering terribly from demon-possession." 23 Jesus did not answer a word. So his disciples came to him and urged him, "Send her away, for she keeps crying out after us." 24 He answered, "I was sent only to the lost sheep of Israel." 25 The woman came and knelt before him. "Lord, help me!" she said. 26 He replied, "It is not right to take the children's bread and toss it to their dogs."27 "Yes, Lord," she said, "but even the dogs eat the crumbs that fall from their masters' table." 28 Then Jesus answered, "Woman, you have great faith! Your request is granted." And her daughter was healed from that very hour. NIV*

e) *James 5:14-16   Is any one of you sick? He should call the elders of the church to pray over him and anoint him with oil in the name of the Lord. 15 And the prayer offered in faith will make the sick person well; the Lord will raise him up. If he has sinned, he will be forgiven. 16 Therefore confess your sins to each other and pray for each other so that you may be healed. The prayer of a righteous man is powerful and effective. NIV*

f) Acts 5:15-16   As a result of the apostles' work, sick people were brought out into the streets on beds and mats so that Peter's shadow might fall across some of them as he went by. 16 Crowds came from the villages around Jerusalem, bringing their sick and those possessed by evil spirits, and they were all healed. NLT

g) Acts 19:11-12   God gave Paul the power to perform unusual miracles. 12 When handkerchiefs or aprons that had merely touched his skin were placed on sick people, they were healed of their diseases, and evil spirits were expelled. NLT

4. *God Heals In Many Ways*

a) Through the Gifted such as the Hunters, K. Kuhlman, Oral Roberts, Fr. DeOrlo, John Wimber, Benny Hinn, Fr. DeGrandis, etc.

b) In His mercy and grace by our petitions.

c) In His mercy and grace through the petitions of others.

d) Sacraments.

e) The Word of God.

f) Praise and worship.

g) Doctors and medicine.

h) God is sovereign and will heal as He chooses, though usually we participate through exercising our faith.

5. ***Tricky Situations***

   a) We are not practicing medicine and do not tell them to discontinue medicine. Their doctor will confirm healing.

   b) We are not doctors, and we believe God sometimes uses doctors as a part of His healing provision. (Luke was a physician.)

   c) Don't override the personhood of the person by telling them they are healed or to claim their healing. That is the Holy Spirit's job. Let them tell you the results and continue with other faith form actions.

   d) Keep your eyes open and observe them while you minister. It is rare that nothing appears to happen…

   Is the Holy Spirit moving upon them? Do you physically feel an anointing?

   Know and declare "God has begun a good work… we bless You, Lord, and thank You for what You are doing."

   You can say honestly "I believe your healing has begun." According to Mark 16:17,18 when we lay hands on the sick, they <u>will</u> *recover*.

   Webster's Dictionary definition of recover: *to regain a normal position or condition, as of health recovering from the effects of a cold* (Notice there is no time element mentioned here. Some recoveries are progressive, and some are immediate.)

   e) Encourage them to receive ministry whenever they can.

   f) Lack of results may indicate presence of emotional hurt, unforgiveness, bitterness, need of inner healing, or a spirit.

- **g.** Word of knowledge or wisdom, and discerning of spirits may be necessary to pinpoint blockage.
- **h.** *Acts 10:38* Jesus was not hindered from healing by unbelief. *"...now He went about doing good and healing all who were under the power of the devil because God was with him."*
- **i.** *Mark 6:5 He could not do any miracles there, except lay his hands on a few sick people and heal them.*
- **j.** Because of unbelief, only a few people came to him for healing, so just the coming can be considered an act of faith.
- **k.** And Jesus, knowing only a few would come, went anyway, because the Individual Is Important to Him—not the numbers.

6. *Prayer of Forgiveness*

Gleaned from teachings of

Fr. DeGrandis and Betty Tapscott

Lord Jesus, today I choose to forgive everyone in my life. I know that You love me more than I love myself. Give me the desire and ability to forgive totally.

Father, I forgive you for the times death, difficulties, or what I thought were punishments sent by You, came into the family. Sometimes people said *"It's God's will,"* and I became bitter and resentful. Cleanse my heart and mind today.

Lord, I forgive MYSELF for my sins, faults and failings. I repent of any delving into horoscopes, going to séances, fortune-telling, wearing lucky charms; I renounce any involvement with new age teaching, channelers, ESP, etc. I forgive myself… Your word says your people perish for lack of knowledge… Give me discernment to recognize the traps of the enemy.

I also forgive myself for taking Your name in vain, not worshipping You in spirit and in truth, not going to church, hurting my parents, abusing alcohol or other substances, indulging in bad books or movies, fornication, adultery, homosexuality, leading children into impurity or abusing them emotionally or physically.

I forgive myself for committing abortion, murder, my part in the war, lying, stealing, defrauding, gossip, slander… I am truly sorry.

I forgive my MOTHER for the times she hurt me, resented me, or punished me too harshly. I forgive her for the times she preferred my brothers or sisters to me. I forgive her for the times she told me I was dumb, stupid, ugly, and the worst of the children, that I cost a lot of money... For the times she told me I was unwanted, a mistake, an accident… and not what she expected... I forgive her.

I forgive my FATHER for any non-support, lack of love, affection, nurturing or attention. I forgive him for not giving me his companionship, for drinking, fighting with my mother and all of us. I forgive him for the physical, emotional, sexual abuse...for severe punishments, for desertion, being away from home...for divorcing my mother or running around...for all these things and any others...I forgive him.

Lord, I extend forgiveness to any SIBLINGS who competed for my parents' love or attention, who hurt me physically, lied about me, rejected me or made life unpleasant for me...I forgive them.

I forgive my SPOUSE for lack of love, affection, consideration, support, attention, communication; for faults, failings, weaknesses and other acts or words that hurt or disturbed me.

I choose to forgive my CHILDREN for their lack of respect, obedience, love, attention, bad habits, substance abuse, sexual permissiveness and sins, falling away from the Lord and the church, and any other acts that disturbed me.

I forgive RELATIVES: aunts, uncles, in-laws, grandchildren... Neighbors... Co-workers... Employers.

I forgive Government Political Parties and Politicians, and religious denominations that harassed, attacked, argued, tried to convert me, forced their views on me, and asked me for money.

I forgive Professional People-doctors, nurses, lawyers and others- who may have hurt me in any way.

I forgive judges, civil servants, and all service people, policemen, bus drivers, medical workers, and repairmen who have taken advantage of me.

I forgive schoolteachers or instructors, who called me dumb, humiliated me, treated me unjustly, or made me stay after school.

Lord, I forgive FRIENDS who have let me down, lost contact with me, who were not there when I needed them, who borrowed money and didn't repay it, or gossiped about me.

I especially pray for the grace to forgive that ONE PERSON in my life who has hurt me the most. I forgive anyone I consider my greatest enemy, the one who is hardest to forgive, or the one I vowed I would never forgive.

Thank You, Jesus. I am free of the evil of unforgiveness. Holy Spirit, fill me with your light and love in every dark area of my heart and mind. **AMEN.**

Matt. 6:14,15 Your heavenly Father will forgive you if you forgive those who sin against you; but if you refuse to forgive them, he will not forgive you.

7. *Satan's battlefields are the mind and body*

A Christian's spirit cannot be touched by Satan

Mind

a) Satan lies: *John 8:44 "He is a liar and the father of lies."*
b) He plants evil thoughts.
c) He accuses: *Rev. 12:10 "For the accuser of our brothers Who accuses them before our God day and Night, has been hurled down."*
d) He condemns: *Rom 8:1 "Therefore, there is no condemnation for those who are in Christ Jesus."*
e) He oppresses: ***Webster defines oppress as: to weigh down, burden in spirit as if with weight. To rule***

cruelly or too severely.

Body

a) Infirming spirits can cause disease, oppression and rob you of life

b) Many times a spirit of death may be present. When in doubt, bind the spirit of Infirmity and command it to depart.

Spirits of infirmity may be

AIDS	*SUBSTANCE ABUSE*
ALLERGIES	*ASTHMA*
ALZHEIMER'S	*BLINDNESS*
CANCERS	*LEPROSY*
LUPUS	*MUSCULAR*
SCLEROSIS	*TUMORS*
CEREBRAL PALSY	*DEPRESSION*
DIABETES	*EPILEPSY*
HERPES	*DEAFNESS*
INSANITY	*LEUKEMIA*
M.S.	*PARKINSONS*
STROKES	*PALSY*

DYSTROPHY

In cases of Ancestral spirits, some may be

Addictions	*Insanity*	*Arthritis*
Divorce	*Allergies*	*Sexual sins*
Perversions	*Diabetes*	*Anger*

Sometimes more than one spirit or kind of spirit is operating

Suggested Deliverance Ministry Model

I bind you Satan in the name of Jesus, and command (Specific spirit) to go by the power of the Holy Spirit, your access to (the person) is broken forever in Jesus Name.

Don't converse with a demonic spirit…the Holy Spirit and you are in charge

Enemy spirits can manifest and try to create fear, confusion, and attention

Bind them and command to be quiet and still In the Name of Jesus.

Don't follow manifestations....follow the Holy Ghost.

8. ***When there seems to be no results***

a) A spirit won't go…they may need teaching.
b) There may be a stronghold of sin, or a problem with someone who committed sin against that person.
c) Lovingly ask if someone hurt them badly and if they need God's help to fully forgive.
d) Don't condemn, accuse or be unkind.
e) Ask the Holy Spirit for Word of Knowledge and Word of Wisdom.
f) Be gentle and respect the person.
g) They may need soul healing through a forgiveness type prayer.

Inner Healing

Any person that has placed all their burdens on the Lord has no need for inner healing. Frances did, and she received and accepted all forgiveness. Some have not taken this step and need teaching to receive God's fullness.

Inner healing Promised

Ps. 147:3 *"He heals the broken hearted and binds up their wounds."*

1 Thess. 5:23 May God Himself, the God of peace, sanctify you through and through. May your whole spirit, soul and body be kept blameless at the coming of our Lord Jesus Christ.

Inner healing is forgiveness, forgiving ourselves, others, God and reconciliation

LISTEN TO THE HOLY SPIRIT

OBEY THE HOLY SPIRIT

TRUST THE HOLY SPIRIT

If a hurt isn't healed, a spirit may be involved. Direct the person to receive ministry from a qualified Inner Healing ministry. Unless you are specifically called, lead, or trained for Inner Healing ministry, do not attempt, except for a prayer similar to the following model:

Inner Healing Prayer, Healing of Memories

Father, I thank You for Your Son, Jesus; Who died on the cross not only for my sins, but for my fears. I thank You that Jesus is the same yesterday, today, and forever, and that He wants me to be completely whole: spirit, soul and body. Lord Jesus, I ask You to walk back through every second of my life, heal me and make me whole. Go back into the third and fourth generations and break harmful genetic ties.

Jesus, You knew all about me even before I was born. Thank You for being there as life began. If fear or any other negative force was transmitted to me as I was in my mother's womb, set me free from those things. Thank You, Lord Jesus, for being there when I was born and for loving me. (Some came into this world not being loved and not being wanted, and they felt rejection). Lord Jesus, from the very beginning, fill each one with Your precious love.

Lord, walk back through every second of my life during those early years. (Some were separated from parents because of sickness or death; some were born into large families and did not receive the love that was needed). Lord Jesus, go back and fill every void, give me the love that was not received. Remove every hurt. Take away all fears: fear of animals, fear of darkness, and fear of falling, fear of being lost. I thank You, Jesus, for setting me free and healing me.

I pray, Lord, that You will take my hand and walk with me to school. At times I felt so shy, so afraid to leave home and go into new situations. Jesus, there were times I felt embarrassment at school; would You please take away those memories? When I was treated harshly by a teacher, or I was hurt by classmates, please heal those hurts. (Some fears entered during those first school years, fear of speaking in public, or fear of failure). Thank You for healing those hurts and setting me free from those fears. I thank You and praise You.

Lord Jesus, I thank you for my mother. (For those who did not have the love of a mother, fill that void, that empty place and give them that love that was needed). I ask you to stand in between my mother and me and let Your divine love flow between us. I ask forgiveness from my mother from any way I have hurt her or failed her, and I forgive her for any way she hurt or failed me.

Lord Jesus, thank you for my Dad. (For those who did not feel love of an earthly dad, please give them all the love they needed but didn't receive). Stand between my dad and me. I pray that Your divine love will mend any broken relationship. I ask forgiveness from my dad for any way I hurt or failed him, and I forgive him for any way he hurt or failed me.

I lift up my brothers and sisters to You. Where there were feelings of competition, jealousy, resentment, I ask that Your healing power mend every broken relationship. I forgive each brother and sister for hurting me. I ask their forgiveness for hurting or failing them.

Thank You, Lord, for being there in my teenage years when I was in junior high school and high school. There were new problems and fears. As each painful memory is brought to my mind, I pray that You will take a spiritual eraser and wipe the pain from my mind. Take away any feeling of humiliation, embarrassment, guilt, fear of failure. (Some have been teased because of race, looks, size, or poverty and they were wounded so deeply). Let each person know You loved them as a special, unique individual and that You were in every situation.

As each of us started to leave home there were new fears, frustrations, or hurts. (Some wanted to go to college and were not able to, others were not able to enter the profession they had dreamed of, and then felt such disappointment). Jesus, please heal every disappointment and every hurt.

Thank You for being there as we entered marriage. (For some, it was such a beautiful, new beginning. For others it was a nightmare). Jesus, take away every hurt. I pray that you would stand in between me and my mate (if there has been more than one mate, please stand in between each one) and heal every hurt. I am saying to my mate, I forgive you for hurting me, and I ask your forgiveness for hurting you. Lord Jesus, through Your divine love, I thank You for melting away every painful memory.

Lord, I thank You for our children. Take away any feeling I have of failure or guilt as a parent. When I punished unwisely or was too possessive with my love, when words were spoken in criticism or anger, I pray You will heal any hurt that was caused. I ask their forgiveness and forgive them for hurting me.

Lord, during those terrifying times of accidents, those times of sickness or surgery, I thank You for being there. I ask You now to take away the horror, the fear, and the memory of the pain. Set me free from the trauma I felt. Thank You for being there during the times of sorrow. I thank You for taking my hand and walking through the valley with me. I thank You for lifting the burden; I thank You for taking away my sorrow, my grief, and my mourning. I thank You for giving me Your joy and Your peace.

Now, Lord Jesus, thank You for walking back through every second of my life up to this moment. Thank You for healing me of all my hurts, my painful memories, and my fears, and for setting me free. Thank You for filling me with Your love. Help me to love myself. Help me to love others. But most of all, Jesus, help me to love You as I desire. I thank You for giving me joy. Thank You Jesus, for giving me peace. I thank You for going way down in deep in the darkest recesses of my mind and cleansing me.

Final Prayer Model for Healing of Memories

Thank You for healing my emotions, my mind, and my memories. I thank You, Jesus, for making me whole, and I give You all the praise and all the glory. In Your name I pray. AMEN.

Suggested Ministry for Generational Bondages

I bind you Satan in the Name of Jesus and by faith place the cross between (person) and his ancestors. The cross breaks the line of inheritance and now all family traits and characteristics must flow through the cross. All the works of the devil are destroyed by the cross and blood lines cleansed by the blood of Jesus. Our inheritance is from our Heavenly Father. We are imprinted with His likeness. We bear His Image. We are adopted into God's Family, so we share His nature. His spirit and His love we release in (person) to become all God created him to be.

Completion of Teaching/Study Outline

Final Remarks

Healing Meeting Agenda may include

- Praise and Worship

- Salvation/Baptism in the Holy Spirit ministry
- Teaching/Demonstration of God's healing power
- Instruct Healing teams/Healing teams ministering to the sick
- Testimonies on stage
- Remember and restate Jesus' commissioning and charge to His disciples
- Give a personal/corporate Commissioning prayer/charge
- Conduct an anointing/commissioning service
- Closing Prayer

Ministry Advice

- Minister in two's or threes
- Minster to same sex or couples plus one
- Seek and be open to Word of Knowledge, Word of Wisdom, and Discerning of Spirits
- Be loving and patient
- Stay away from mysticism, hypnotism, mind control techniques, etc.
- Stay in peace and in the Anointing.
- Be totally submitted (spirit and soul) to and under authority.

After ministering to a person tell them they can return to their seat. If the person has had a dramatic and obvious healing, direct them or bring them to the platform to share their testimony. If a person does not have an immediate healing, do not send them to the Crawford's. Leave the person with a word of encouragement. God often heals over a period of time. All healings are not immediate.

Today, you are the ministers God will use. As ministers, keep a proper attitude, pray in tongues, listen to all instructions from the platform, be flexible, be bold and remain in the Spirit at all times.

Forgiveness is what Christianity is.

The Happy Hunters: Charles and Frances Hunter

By Paul Crawford

We have had the privilege of working with many of the great ministries in the world. None has impacted, taught or trained us like the Happy Hunters. Today they are in home stretch of ministry and life. I went with them to Joel Osteen's church and then had lunch, with them, in October 2008. Frances was sharp as a tack especially for being for 93 years old. She had just read our book and they were proud of their spiritual offspring.

Charles and Frances are always the same. Whether on the platform at a healing explosion, in a restaurant, at the airport, solving crises, in church, their office or at home they were the same. What you see is what you get. They had differences over some things but always submitted their selves one to another.

Their entire premise of their ministry is "If Charles and Frances can do it you can to." They are equippers, encouragers, imparters and full of love. Their life has been devoted to "Building the Body of Christ". The enormity of what they have accomplished is a blessing to the nations.

One project I helped them accomplish was the recording of 15 hours teaching from the Gospel of John in Russian. I set up my 3 camera system in their Houston auditorium. I had facilitated a trip for them to the Ukraine where the met pastor Henry who spoke Russian and English. Henry was brought to Houston as the interpreter. Frances taught and we recorded 15 hours. I developed a system where 2 master recordings were made. One had both English and Russian interpreted phase by phrase. The other had the English with the Russian electronically removed. This was then sent to China and other nations where Chinese or other languages could be added on phrase by phrase.

Charles and Frances placed 60 video duplicators in St. Petersburg, Russia with a networking ministry. Thousands of 15 hour sets were duplicated and distributed. The Russian military authorized and requested that one set each be placed with all 800 military bases.

The last time they came to Seattle, prior to 9-11, I met them at the airport. Over 300 Russians were there to greet them as a result of their books and video tapes. This happened at every city they visited until 9-11 stopped meeting travelers at the gate.

Our ministry is the results of their ministry. We love and respect them very much.

I thought you would like to know more about them, the enormity and success of their ministry. To do this, I submitted a list of 15 questions to Frances. Her own words speak so powerfully I thought it best for you to see her reply:

1. <u>My event communicating with Charles, prior to and then marrying him</u>?

    Charles had called me on the telephone, and I just fluffed him off, thinking he was just like a lot of the other men in churches that wanted to marry me since I was a widow and had brought our little church up to such great numbers that every pastor had somebody special they wanted me to meet.

    When Charles called me, after the third call, I finally called him back. He asked me to stay at his house. He said he told me that his wife had just died and he would move to a local hotel and I could have the house. But all I heard was that he wanted me to stay at his house. So the first thing I ever said about my beloved husband was, "That dirty old man---who does he think he is and who does he think I am?"

    When I met him in Houston, on an evangelistic trip there, I thought, "I'll freeze him out." However, something wonderful happened when Charles and I shook hands---not a word came out of either one of our mouths---we just looked at each other and our spirits leapt between us And 88 days later we were married because God spoke to us and told us the exact time, minute, and place to be married.

We had no dates. We never saw each other from the time we met. We even missed each other in the airport when Charles came to claim me as his bride. But we will be celebrating our 39th perfect, perfect wedding anniversary on January 1, 2009.

2.   <u>When was the first big arena Healing Explosion and how many attended?</u>

The first big Healing Explosion was held in Pittsburgh, Pennsylvania on July 4, 1985 at the Pittsburgh Civic Arena and there were approximately 12,000 people attending.

3.   <u>How many big arenas Healing Explosions was there</u>?

We have had 172 Healing Explosions in bigger arenas, and "He" was there in every one of them.

4.   <u>Largest, excluding the Astrodome?</u>

The largest one is difficult to say because we had many Healing Explosions in South America where we ran over 60,000 people and then they locked thousands outside the door.

5. <u>The first World Event in the Astrodome?</u>

The first World Event at the Astrodome was a Billy Graham meeting, and we had the last World Event there.

6. <u>How many books published to date?</u>

We have had 60 books published to date.

7. <u>How many "How to Heal the Sick" distributed?</u>

There have been millions of copies of "How to Heal the Sick" distributed in many different languages. Many of the countries just automatically reprint your books without your permission, so we have no way of knowing altogether how many have been distributed.

8. <u>Best Seller after "How to Heal the Sick"?</u>

The best seller after "How to Heal the Sick" would be "God's Answer to Fat," and "Hotline to Heaven." Both of these made the No. 1 Best Seller List.

9. <u>"How to Heal the Sick" in what languages?</u>

"How to Heal the Sick" has been printed in many languages that we don't even know about. However, some of the ones that we know positively, because we have copies of them, are Dutch, French, German, Hungarian, Japanese, Korean, Polish, Portuguese, Romanian, Russian, Spanish, Swahili, and Ukrainian.

10. "How to Heal the Sick" video school—what languages?

In every country where books have been translated, they have also been translated video schools.

11. How many videos distributed in Russia?

We have distributed thousands of videos in the Ukraine and in Russia. But to give you an exact count is impossible.

12. World census description and grand total?

God spoke to us to take a census of the world. And when we finally finished the count, the total number of salvations was 1,000,626,754.

Hunter's had teams in many nations, which went door to door, asking a question about their place with God. Some nations every home, where it was practicable, was visited and the count is those that sad a sinners prayer.

13. How and when did you personalize the scriptures?

God spoke to me one morning when I was reading the Bible, and I thought a particular portion did not apply to me because He was talking to Paul at that time. But God spoke and said, "I was talking to you." So ever since that time, which was probably in 1968, I have made my Bible a personal Bible.

14. How many times you have ministered?

There is no way to estimate how many times we have ministered. However, to give you an approximate number, which would just be a wild guess on my part; it would be over 20,000 times. We have ministered in 49 different foreign countries around the world.

15. Give an endorsement for the book?

We would be very happy to give you an endorsement of the book. Anytime you are ready, let me know.

In some instances you will notice I had to be tremendously vague because I really have no way of going back and checking.

In His Love,

Charles and Frances Hunter